THE CULTURE LOVER'S GUIDE TO

MADRID

For Sarah, my love, remembering our dawn walks on Rosales

All photographs Callum Moy

THE CULTURE LOVER'S GUIDE TO MADRID

CALLUM MOY

WHITE OWL
AN IMPRINT OF PEN & SWORD BOOKS LTD.
YORKSHIRE – PHILADELPHIA

First published in Great Britain in 2025 by
White Owl
An imprint of
Pen & Sword Books Ltd.
Yorkshire - Philadelphia

ISBN 978 1 03610 555 6

A CIP catalogue record for this book is available from the British Library.

Design: SJmagic DESIGN SERVICES, India.

The Publisher's authorised representative in the EU for product safety is Authorised Rep Compliance Ltd., Ground Floor, 71 Lower Baggot Street, Dublin D02 P593, Ireland.
www.arccompliance.com

For a complete list of Pen & Sword titles please contact

PEN & SWORD BOOKS LIMITED
George House, Beevor Street, Off Pontefract Road, Hoyle Mill, Barnsley, South Yorkshire, England, S71 1HN.
E-mail: enquiries@pen-and-sword.co.uk
Website: www.pen-and-sword.co.uk

or

PEN AND SWORD BOOKS
1950 Lawrence Rd, Havertown, PA 19083, USA
E-mail: uspen-and-sword@casematepublishers.com
Website: www.penandswordbooks.com

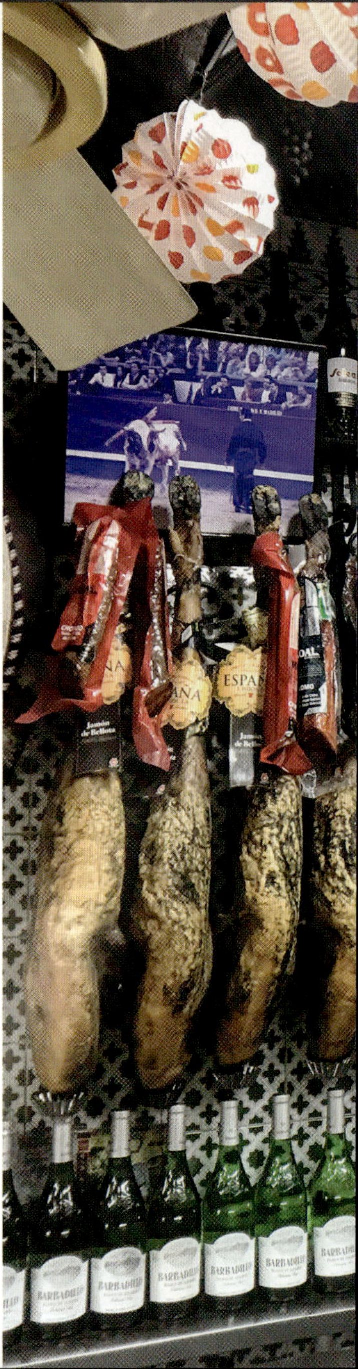

CONTENTS

1

INTRODUCTION

In the centre of Spain – according to the Kilometre Zero stone slab in Puerta de Sol – Madrid sits at an elevation of 657 metres, giving it the most unique climate of any European capital. Cold winters, at times bitterly so, and scorching summers make it an unlikely location for a capital created 500 years ago at the whim of King Philip II, mainly to escape ecclesiastical oversight in Toledo. It would take more than 300 years, until 1885, before Pope Leo XIII finally intervened to instruct the Catholic Church of Spain to permit Madrid its own bishopric, thereby allowing the city a cathedral.

Conflict, whether religious, military or political, has long been a feature of life in Madrid. Spain's fertile coastal land, sea ports and more temperate conditions made it a prized possession for Mediterranean, north European and African cultures. It is the capital that beat all others to South America – and so reaped the rewards and consequences of the wealth that poured in from Mexico and Peru. Around the same time, whilst the British opened up inhospitable Newfoundland (and exported cod) Spain extracted silver, estimated to be around 150,000 tonnes, until sources were depleted.

The influx of precious metal had long-term consequences: a disinterest in, and moreover destruction of, indigenous industry, an attitude of invincibility in world affairs and the creation of an unequal society – too concerned with 'hand kissing and royal intrigues' in the words of Manuel Azana (Prime Minister of the Second Republic 1931, and President 1937–39). The two worlds of central Madrid can be seen today in the destitute of Vallecas and the affluent of Salamanca – descendants of the courtiers, chancers and rogues that arrived in the capital in the hope of advancement.

With wealth came demand for the finer things in life: grand architecture, visual arts, fashion (*haute couture* and mass-market), literature and the performing arts – all evident on the streets today. But, strangely not gastronomy, unless you are a fan of the traditional chickpea-based meat stew (Cocido), potato omelette and tripe dishes so loved by Madrileños.

Plaza de Cibeles from the Terraza Cibeles.

Jardines del Descubrimiento.

The arts and eating and drinking out are much in evidence in Madrid today. Europe's largest concentration of paintings in the so-called 'Golden Triangle' (centred on Museo Nacional del Prado) draws millions to the city each year. And *Lonely Planet* reported that Madrid ranks fourth in the world for city-centre bar numbers (behind London, Tokyo and New York City) but, importantly for locals, not Barcelona!

Young Madrileños are city people, although the agrarian-based afternoon siesta is still a protected time even in the height of winter. Unlike the British, they do not hanker after the country life, associating it with relentless heat, toil and poverty. Instead, commercial opportunities, consumer pleasures (denied to their grandparents), long nights and late rises dictate the pace of life. As Elizabeth Nash comments in *Madrid*, the city is probably more appreciated by the dedicated urbanite.

This book introduces the reader to the culture of Madrid, its principal historical sights and a selection of its most 'castizo' (i.e., authentic) bars and restaurants, all to be savoured with a wine and tapas in hand. I hope the reader will visit many of the locations to experience Madrid's culture and see where much of modern Spanish history took place.

2

ORIGINS

Ancient history

The first human findings on the Iberian Peninsula date from around 1.5 million years ago with evidence of (palaeolithic) hunter gatherer and fishing communities. The species evolved to Neanderthals (250,000 years ago) before being extinguished by Homo Sapiens around 40,000 years ago. Immigration increased during the ice age (i.e., 22,000 to 14,000BC) as harsh conditions in northern Europe drove humans and animals south into warmer Spain, which never iced over. Cave paintings throughout Spain, evidence of thought, are testament to this influx of people, but none are near Madrid. The absence of coastal resources, harsher weather and a trickling river made the environment unattractive for early settlers. Spain's famed 'Golden Age' poet Francisco Quevedo would later describe Madrid's River Manzanares as an apprentice stream!

During the neolithic period (4200 to 2200BC), the area of Madrid became more populated and by 1000BC, farming, pottery making and cloth weaving were well established by Celt Iberian tribes, living in stable settlements. Over the next 500 years, while seeking and finding metals (particularly tin), the more advanced Phoenician followed by Greek civilisations invaded the Iberian Peninsula from the east across the Mediterranean, occupying the south and north respectively. They brought a host of advances to the peninsula, including weights and measures, olives, grapes, grains, societal hierarchy and new belief systems, all absorbed by the indigenous tribes. Phoenicians founded Seville, Cadiz and Malaga whilst the Greeks founded Barcelona. But neither civilisation settled permanently, and the Phoenicians preferred the north African coast where they later established the Carthaginian Empire.

The Phoenician, Greek and indigenous civilisations were subsequently displaced by the Romans, who arrived from around 200BC. But, unique for European capitals, there are no Roman remains in Madrid – again the coastal resources and climate being more favoured. So, Madrid is hardly a bucket-list destination for classicists, except for an original Egyptian temple gifted to the city in modern times.

The **Temple of Debod** (C. de Ferraz) is located on an infamous site of bloodshed (formerly known as Mount Principe Pio); first during the War of Independence in the early 1800s and then as location of the Montana Barracks during the Spanish Civil War between 1936–39. The temple dates from around 200BC. Built by a Pharoh for the God Anun and Goddess Isis, it's a popular tourist destination with an outstanding display of Egyptian decorative motifs, and uses scale models and videos to bring to life the magnificence. The temple was gifted to Spain by the Egyptian government as thanks for Spain's assistance in the construction of the Aswan Dam and to otherwise save it from destruction when the valley was flooded.

Eating and drinking: The ubiquitous tapas is a complimentary snack, originally a piece of bread placed over a glass to prevent insects and dust from entering, provided as a thank you for your patronage. Paid dishes are larger plates, sometimes called tapas or aperitivo, whilst raciones are more substantial meals. A pintxos is also a paid snack, usually held together with a cocktail stick, used to calculate what you owe at the end. Madrid's signature snack is the 'bocadillos de calamares' – a baguette with fried squid and no butter. It originates from when fish (important on Fridays and during Lent) was not plentiful owing to the distance of Madrid from the sea. Calamares were caught and fried in Valencia and remained in good condition upon arrival in Madrid.

The morning staple is café con leche with toast and a tomato-based sauce. Whilst the evening is often kicked off with a cerveza, in descending sizes of a jarra, doble or cana, or a jarra of sangria, before moving on to national or local wines. Naturally, there are many wines to choose from, including reds from Ribera del Duero and La Mancha and whites from Albarino and Verdejo, all complimented by the local Manchego cheese. You might end the night with a gin and tonic, enjoyed as a digestive rather than an aperitive.

Popular raciones are Cocido Madrileño (a chickpea and meat-based stew), Callos Madrileños (stewed tripe) or a dish of fried pig's ear. Alternatively, you may want to stick with Croquetas con Jamon, Tortilla, Bacalao (i.e., fried cod pieces) or the ubiquitous Heuvos Rotos (i.e., ham, egg and chips). Naturally, restaurants offer abundant alternatives, drawing on the rich produce, sea food (both pescados y mariscos) and meat stocks nurtured throughout the country. Since a tapa (pl. tapas) is intended as a complementary snack with your drink, wait to see if it is provided, rather than immediately ordering food. Away from the tourist spots, it invariably is.

Local eats

Near the Temple of Debod, **Rosales 20** (Paseo del Pintor Rosales) is a stylish bar and a restaurant serving international and Spanish dishes and with a chic interior design. Also, very good for watching televised football over a drink.

Madrid's **Museo de San Isidro,** near the buzzing district of La Latina, is a superb exposition of early Madrid, covering its ancient history and beginnings with comprehensive captions in English. A three-dimensional model of Madrid during the early nineteenth century helps to orient the visitor to the growth of Madrid from its Arab foundations to Habsburg and Bourbon prominence. Furthermore, the museum itself is on the site where Madrid's patron saint (San Isidro Labrador) worshipped and died. For a week in the middle of May (around the 15th), Madrid celebrates

Rosales 20.

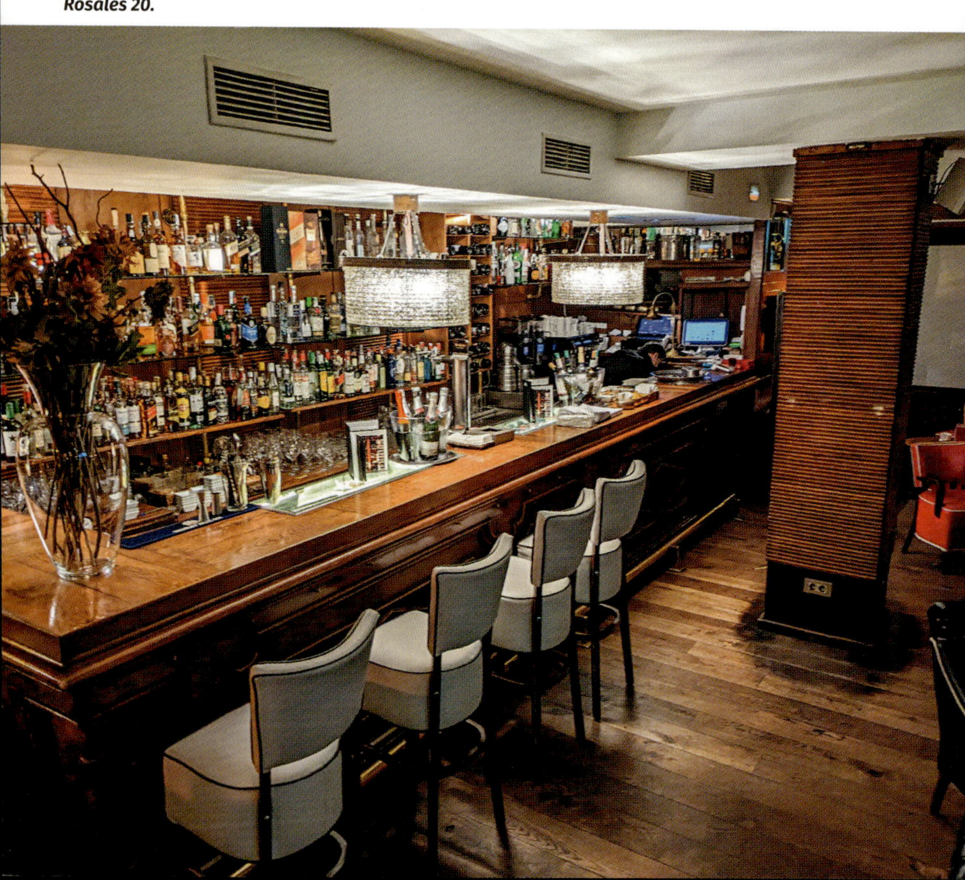

San Isidro with its largest city-wide festival of free concerts, events and activities for the family.

Local eats

Juana La Loco (taking its name from the daughter of the Catholic Monarchs) is a stylish bistro offering a selection of classic Spanish and European fare – reputedly offering the finest tortilla made with or without onions, this being a point of heated debate among Madrileños.

Viuda de Vacas (C. del Aguila) is a late nineteenth-century tavern serving Spanish cuisine. Tucked away from the bustle of nearby La Latina, the locale has a film-set feel to it and is off the tourist track.

Temple of Debod.

Museo de San Isidro.

Viuda de Vacas.

San Isidro Festival, Paseo del Quince de Mayo.

3

CONFLICT AND CONQUEST

Consolidation

The arrival of the Roman Empire in the Iberian Peninsula resulted from struggles for dominance in the western Mediterranean with the Carthaginian Empire, located in what is Tunisia today. Despite the efforts of Hannibal in leading a force across the Strait of Gibraltar up through Spain and into Italy during the so-called Punic Wars, Carthage succumbed to Rome in 149BC.

The first signs of Roman colonisation date from around 219BC, mainly along the coast and principal rivers, delineated by the River Ebro in the north east, which marked the boundary with the Roman province of Gaul. The Romans left a rich infrastructure of public works in Spain, most evident at Tarragona and Cartegna (on the east coast), Merida (in the west) and the astounding aqueduct in Segovia, the closest major Roman remains to Madrid. Rome also bequeathed a common language, institutions like the law and municipality and not least Christianity in its later years (i.e., late AD 300). Under Roman occupation, mining, farming, fishing and salting industries were developed on a large scale. Spain's main exports to Rome were metals, olive oil and grain – plus the Emperors Trajan and Hadrian and the early convert to Christianity St Lawrence, all of Spanish descent.

After considerable resistance from Celtic tribes, in 139BC the Romans conquered Complutum and Alcala de Henares, both to the east of Madrid. But Madrid never acquired any importance, other than as a crossroads to all points with a small settlement at Carpetania sustained by the River Manzanares. Pressure in the homeland from Germanic peoples (i.e., the Goths, Huns and Vandals) forced Rome to withdraw its forces from its far-flung provinces almost overnight. Once the Romans left in the fifth century the Manzanares was abandoned.

In Spain, the Visigoths ably filled the power vacuum, establishing the Christian capital of the Visigothic kingdom at the strategic location of

Toledo. Surrounded by large land estates, it was controlled by oligarchies who offered safety and food in return for allegiance and work. It was the beginnings of Spain's feudal model that prospered well into the nineteenth century with power shared between the king, aristocracy and church – a model that shaped development up to modern times.

From the fifth century, the village of Madrid became a small settlement. But there are no *in situ* remains of the infrastructure or art from this period, although the Museo Arqueologico Nacional displays Visigothic treasures from other parts of Spain.

An outstanding story of Spain's pre-history, early history, Roman and Visigothic foundations and artefacts is on display at the **Museo Arqueologico Nacional**. The museum, founded during the reign of Queen Isabella II in 1867, and boasting stunning classical architecture and modern interiors, is home to archaeological exhibits, mostly excavated in Spain, plus the unmissable reconstruction of Spain's famous cave paintings at Altamira. Full captions in English add enormously to a visit. Nearby, founded in 1712, the **Biblioteca Nacional de Espana** greets visitors with large statues of Spanish national and literary heroes (e.g., San Isidro, King Pelayo and Miguel Cervantes). It is Spain's equivalent to the British Library, albeit pre-dating it by 50 years. The public cannot access the reading rooms without prior registration, but can enter the resplendent entrance hall, ascend the lavish marble staircase, visit the committee room and attend several free exhibitions in the main building and basement annex.

Local eats

Restaurante Ultramarinos Quintín (C. de Jorge Juan) is a Mediterranean-style restaurant on three floors, popular with stylish locals in the heart of the Salamanca neighbourhood.

Biblioteca Nacional de Espana.

Museo Arqueologico Nacional.

Restaurante Ultramarinos Quintin.

The first age of enlightenment

Suffering incursions from other north European tribes, the Visigoths made a soft invitation to the north African Moors (of Arabic Syrian descent) to assist in quelling these invasions. Only too willing to help, in 711 General Tariq crossed the Strait of Gibraltar with thousands of troops, setting up a bridgehead in Gibraltar (meaning the 'mountain of Tariq' in Arabic). By 719 the Moors had captured all of Spain – only being stopped at Covadonga (in the far north) by the Spanish and at Tours by the French. Spain would spend the next 800 years seeking to recover the lands lost.

By the mid-700s, Prince Abd al-Rahman I proclaimed himself emir of the Caliphate Al-Andalus (i.e., independent of Syria) with its capital at Cordoba. Arabs still refer to the whole of Spain as Al-Andalus.

The Moors brought innovative methods of farming and irrigation, a well-developed crafts industry and a flourishing culture. And by 950, Cordoba, with a population of approximately 100,000, became the largest urban centre in Europe. Under the twin pillars of Arabic and Islam, Hispano-Muslim scholars re-adopted classical philosophy and made advances in the understanding and practice of medicine, mathematics, astronomy and the decorative arts. In 961, Hakam III had compiled a library of several thousands of volumes – a feat unmatched elsewhere in Europe.

Trade with north Africa was at the foundation of Muslim Spain's hegemony. By eight hundred, Madrid was selected as a suitable location to protect trade routes running north between Toledo and Alcala de Henares. Atop a hill, with a river and plentiful underground water, Madrid was a strategic location – and derived its name from the Arabic word Majrit (i.e., place of abundant water). By 850, under the Emir Mohamed I, the site was fortified with an Alcazar, occupying the present location of the Palacio Real (i.e., Royal Palace). The city followed the pattern of many Muslim settlements comprising a fortress with a central medina and a labyrinth of narrow and winding streets surrounded by a defensive wall – a format, albeit enlarged, that lasted to the end of the 1800s (by then, mainly to control the spread of disease and for taxation).

The **Muralla Arabe** is the oldest surviving part of Madrid. Discovered in 1953, it is believed the wall was built between 854 and 871 to defend against incursions from the Christians from Asturias (i.e., northern Spain) and uprisings in Toledo. It is the oldest Islamic wall in Spain and a national monument. The remains of the wall are best viewed from within the landscaped **Parque del Emir Mohamed I**.

Local eats

Nearby **Café del Monaguillo** (Pl. de la Cruz Verde) serves café fare, paella and grilled meats which can be taken on the

The development of Madrid, Muralla Arabe.

Parque del Emir Mohamed I and the Muralla Arabe.

Cafe del Monaguillo.

attractive fountain-enhanced terrace. Uniquely, the café also boasts an extensive library of inexpensive used books for sale.

Plaza de la Paja is Madrid's oldest square, originally laid out in 850. It was Madrid's civic and commercial centre until construction started on Plaza Mayor in the 1570s. Today, it is an off the tourist trail pedestrianised square surrounded by bars and restaurants and large plane trees. A walled rose-garden, the **Jardin del Principe Anglona** (once a bishop's garden) on the south side of the square is a quieter spot.

Local eats

El Viva (C. de San Andres) is one of a handful of café/restaurants facing Plaza de la Paja. It specialises in good value sandwiches, and the traditional must-try Madrileño favourite: Pan con Tomate.

Plaza de la Paja.

La Reconquista

The drawn-out reclamation of former Spanish lands (i.e., La Reconquista) started in the mountains around Covadonga in northern Spain, where the much-celebrated King Pelayo of Asturias halted and defeated the Moors in 722.

Throughout the 800–1000s, intense pressure and conquests from Christians in the north, and stifling Arab taxes promoting disunity among Muslim leaders, started to weaken the state and ultimately break up the Caliphate by the early 1000s. In an act of self-harm, the Moors pushed any Christians and Jews north into the Christian territories, thereby depleting sources of wealth and taxation.

In the 900s, King Alfonso III advanced from Oviedo to Leon and later united with the Kingdom of Castile. In 1083, Madrid fell to Alfonso VI. In the last moments of the assault, folklore suggests that a Christian soldier bravely scrambled up the Muslim walls, leapt over and opened the gate. Somebody said, 'look how he moved, just like a cat.' A cat is called a 'gato' in Spanish and the moniker stuck. Today, gato is the name given to any Madrid-born reveller, but with the condition that all four grandparents were also born in the city!

Madrid's city streets were renamed with Christian references, whilst trade guilds and employment were established. During this period, Muslims were forced to live outside the city walls, around Plaza de la Paja.

In 1202, Madrid was granted self-governing powers from Toledo and it became one of the locations for court gatherings and hunting on the iterant circuit of the Castilian kings. By the 1100s, the city's wealthy and connected leaders (i.e., burghers) would meet with nobility and clergy to agree taxation and practices for city-wide management in assemblies still called Cortes today.

On the Atlantic side of the peninsula, the Kingdom of Portugal was established in 1143. As the border with Muslim Spain was pushed further south, the four main Christian kingdoms emerged as Castile, Portugal, Navarre and Aragon-Catalonia. And by the mid-1200s, the Nasrid kingdom of Granada was all that remained of Muslim Spain.

As Madrid grew it established its own parliament in the 1300s, gaining full autonomy from Toledo in the 1400s. Royals stayed at the Alcazar more frequently and began to enhance it architecturally. Christians relied heavily on the building and decorative skills of the Muslims living in their community and a contemporary style of architecture evolved that blended Muslim and Christian influences. Known as the Mudejar style, it combines the square towers and decorative motifs favoured by Muslims and the rounded towers used by the Christians. (NB: Muslims living in Christian territory were called Mudejares, whilst Christians living in Arab territory were called Mozarabs.)

Granada finally fell to the Christians in 1492 under the joint monarchy of Ferdinand II of Aragon and Isabella I of Castile. After nearly 800 years of warfare, the reconquest of the peninsula was a key moment, not just for Spain but all Christian Europe, many at the time seeing it as a payback for the loss of Constantinople to the Turks in 1453. It is a victory that still sits foremost in the consciousness of many Spaniards today, calling on them to support the virtues of Christianity and country-wide unification.

The Christians enlarged the Muslim city and expanded the walls accordingly. The walls are long gone but the location of the gates is remembered through plazas, e.g., Plaza de Santa Domingo, Puerta del Sol and **Plaza de Puerta Cerrada**, where you can read the Madrid city motto inscribed on an adjacent wall, declaring: 'On water I was built, my walls are made of fire.' Thought to have been introduced in the 1100s, it refers to the flint walls, which would spark when hit by arrows, built above the city's water springs. The flint stone can still be seen in the fabric of many older city-centre buildings such as the Real Monasterio de la Encarnacion.

Local eats

Casa Revuelta (C. de Latoneros) is an unassuming café and bistro with a loyal following of Madrileños, manifested by a long queue at the weekends, especially on Sundays.

Plaza de Puerta Cerrada.

There are few Mudejar style buildings remaining in Madrid. The best example is the **Torre de los Lujanes** in Plaza de la Villa, dating from the 1400s and apparently where Francis I of France was kept captive following defeat at the Battle of Pavia in 1525.

With the foundations of its Mudejar tower, dating from the 1300s, the church of **San Pedro el Viejo** stands on the site of an old mosque and is a reminder that the Moors still lived in Madrid around that time.

San Pedro el Viejo.

El Madrono.

Local eats

El Madrono (Pl. de Puerta Cerrada) is a buzzing tapas bar, with a cadre of ebullient waiters. Its mezzanine restaurant is a good bet when other local venues are packed.

Growth of empire

The need to control entry to the Mediterranean and the Spanish coast drove technical advances in ship construction, astronomy and navigation. These skills, plus the Spanish state's desire to keep pace with Portugal, made it both feasible and necessary to launch an expedition seeking the Orient via a western maritime route. Portugal was already reaping the rewards of trade in spices and silks via its well-armed eastern maritime route around the tip of Africa – but was suffering under attacks from English, French and Dutch fleets, all seeking to muscle in on the spice trade. Spain's possession of the Canary Islands provided a station from which to launch the route west in search of the Orient. In 1492, already quite a year for the Catholic Monarchs having just reunified Spain, they funded the voyage of the Italian explorer Christopher

Columbus (Cristobal Colon in Spanish). After ten weeks, on 12 October 1492, the small flotilla arrived at San Salvador Island in the Bahamas and established what would become known as the New World. To his dying day, Columbus believed he had arrived in India.

In 1494, Pope Alexander VI weighed in to resolve the ongoing maritime disputes of Portugal and Spain. The Pope decreed that Portugal should control all routes to the east, to trade with the Orient, whilst Spain would control all routes to the west. Portugal also successfully argued it should be granted the Cape Verde islands (west of Africa) to provide a refuge *en route* south to the tip of Africa – thereby avoiding the need to hug the west coast of Africa and risk the dangerous currents. Later, in 1506, it was agreed the line of longitude could be moved a further 1,200 miles west, to accommodate Portugal's earlier discovery of Brazil – giving it a 400-year permit to exploit and colonise that land, becoming the primary source of the world's gold.

By the 1520s Spain exported Spanish goods to Mexico, shipped them overland to the west coast, then loaded the goods onto Spanish galleons to trade with the Spice islands and China. This was the so-called Tierra Firme Fleet. Along with its Mediterranean fleet warding off the Turks, these were Spain's key maritime trade arteries.

In South America, Spain adopted a policy of divide and conquer, making allies of marginalised tribal leaders. Spain's comparative technical advances made conquest easy. Not only did the indigenous cultures of Mexico and Peru have no firepower, but they also lacked horses and the wheel. Piece by piece the Empire laid claim to, among others, the lands of the Aztecs 'The Viceroyalty of New Spain' (i.e., Mexico, conquered by Cortes in 1521), the Incas 'The Viceroyalty of Peru' (conquered by Pizarro in 1533), and Florida (conquered by Desoto in 1539). Gold was not discovered, but abundant silver was extracted by indigenous labour – many killed either by the sheer toil or use of mercury in processing. Silver was particularly valued as it was traded for Chinese silk, where authorities had decided that silver was the only reliable form of country-wide taxation. Chinese silk flowed into Spain causing hyper-inflation and destroying any indigenous Spanish production of the fibre.

On the other side of the world the Spanish fleet, led by Alvaro de Bazan, crushed the Ottomans at the Battle of Lepanto near Greece in 1571 and once and for all removed the Muslim threat in the Mediterranean. With such wealth and hegemony, Spain could confidently proceed on a war-footing with all-comers.

Located near Plaza de Colon, the **Jardines del Descubrimiento** recall the discovery of America by Columbus. Voyages of other Spanish-funded ventures during the Golden Age are commemorated on the brutalist plinths by architect, Joaquin Vaquero

Jardines del Descubrimiento.

Statue of Christopher Columbus, Jardines, del Descubrimiento.

Turcois. The discovery of America is a contentious claim today, but opened in 1970 the site manages to avoid controversy or cause much introspection about the nation's role in south America. The world's largest Spanish flag is erected at the centre of the garden and a late nineteenth century Columbus column celebrates the achievement in the centre of the plaza. Beneath the gardens, the **Fernan Gomez Cultural Centre** continues the theme with a sculpted mural of the Atlantic voyages and temporary exhibitions on various New World related subjects.

Local eats

Mercado de la Paz (C. de Ayala) is a fashionable food market, frequented by well-healed Salamanca locals for

Mercado de la Paz.

Casa Dani.

their daily produce. It is also home to a variety of bars and eateries. Among them **Casa Dani** is a buzzing place to visit, whilst watching the vendors prepare their gourmet offerings.

At the centre of Plaza de la Villa stands an 1891 marble and bronze statue of **Alvaro de Bazan**, by Mariano Benlliure, remembered for his leadership at Lepanto (above) but also his premature death. Bazan and Philip II disagreed on the strategy to invade England and this may have caused his death in February 1588, just five months before the doomed Spanish Armada set off with the sea-sick suffering Duke of Medina Sidonia at the helm. If Bazan had lived, the outcome for England may have been radically different. England and Spain settled their dispute in 1604, with the Treaty of London.

The **Museo Naval** on Paseo del Prado is located at the Navy General Headquarters. It features around 10,000 items comprising models, maps, instruments, weapons and arts from the medieval period to the present day. One of the most outstanding exhibits

Alvaro de Bazan, Plaza de la Villa.

MUSEO
NAVAL

Museo Naval.

is an enormous wall-map of the American continent – the first known representation of its kind, having been produced by Juan de la Cosa in 1500 after three voyages to America with Christopher Columbus.

In the northern suburb of Moncloa, the **Museo de America** displays an

Museo de America.

Faro de Moncloa from Parque del Oeste.

archaeological and ethnographical history of the Americas in an impressive neo-colonial style building, built in 1954. Its many rooms trace the voyages of the great explorers, artefacts from the lands discovered, and colonial pieces. Consider taking the audio guide since the panels are in Spanish only. Next door the **Faro de Moncloa** (Moncloa Lighthouse) is a 92m-high observation deck with stunning views of the Sierra de Guadarrama and the city.

The **Casa Mexico** in the district of Chamberi serves as cultural exchange between Mexico and Spain, and supports the active integration of Mexicans to the country. Exhibitions, events and a well-stocked bookshop make it a very popular destination. Opened in 2018 and housed in a mansion from the early 1900s, it is run by the Mexican Embassy.

Local eats

Bodegas el Mano (C. de la Palma) is a stylish and affordable restaurant catering to local professionals wanting atmospheric and easy dining. Its location, in the west of Malasana, keeps the tourists away. **Café Comercial** (Gta. de Bilbao) opened in 1887 and is

Café Comercial.

Madrid's oldest literary cafe. It was a place for lively political debate during the Bourbon Restoration, discreet conversation following the Spanish Civil War and the glitzy intrigues of film stars of the '50s and '60s (the cafe was a favourite of Ava Gardner). Today, it is an upmarket bar and restaurant with a thriving cultural programme.

Decline and fall of Empire

The dynastic union of the Habsburgs and House of Burgundy in the low countries, that gave Spain control of the Netherlands, started to be challenged in 1568 – fuelled by growing Dutch nationalism and Protestantism. Spain's attitude of 'silver-fuelled' invincibility resulted in an 80-year long war ending, despite Spanish successes like the Siege of Breda, with the creation of an independent Dutch Republic in 1648 (formed out of the Protestant northern provinces of the Netherlands) and ratified by the Treaty of Westphalia. Not satisfied with the struggle in the low countries, Philip II's aggressive foreign policy also brought Spain into conflict with England, France, the Ottomans and Portugal.

The Kingdom of Portugal (independent since 1143) came under Spanish rule in 1580, when a dynastic crisis (i.e., absence of heirs) and a weakening of its commercial trade by French, Dutch and English maritime incursions, opened the door for Philip II to become the King of Portugal (on account of his mother's Portuguese heritage). Philip II's unpopularity was enhanced by the milking of Portugal to fund the religious 30-year war (1618–48) and from 1640 Portugal fought for its independence, finally achieving this in 1668 and being ratified by the Treaty of Lisbon.

The last gasp of Spanish power in Europe was sealed (during the reign of Philip IV) by the Treaty of the Pyrenees in 1659 that ceded its hegemony to the French kingdom of Louis XIV – itself to become the template for monarchical rule in continental Europe. During the eighteenth century, Spain mostly sought to maintain its neutrality, as it watched from the sidelines as England and France fought it out for commercial supremacy and colonial footholds.

In 1796, Spain formed an alliance with France aimed at attacking Portugal – Britain's ally (and still the world's oldest alliance today). Spain's alliance with France continued into the Napoleonic Wars with disastrous consequences for Spain – not only losing its fleet at the Battle of Trafalgar in 1805, but more fundamentally, losing its independence between 1808–14.

Despite depletion of its finances, Spain still retained its colonies and possessions in Latin America and the control of Naples. But the crisis brought on by the War of Independence awoke feelings of nationalism and freedom among the Spanish colonies. Spain, without a strong maritime fleet and its shipyards depleted of funds, was helpless as the colonies declared independence.

Independence leaders such as Simón Bolívar hastened the demise of the Spanish Empire, as colony after colony fell like ten-pins: Venezuela (1811), Mexico (1821), Peru (1821) and Bolivia (1825). Until in 1898 in humiliating engagements with the United States Navy, Cuba, Puerta Rica, Guam and the Philippines were all ceded to the US (with a cash sweetener of $20 million) and ratified by the Treaty of Paris the same year. The 'shock of 1898', when the Empire was reduced to the mother country, is an event that Spain has struggled to deal with, even up to modern times among those on the political right.

Not unsurprisingly, the fall of the Spanish Empire is not something widely celebrated throughout Madrid. However, many monuments in Madrid's Parque del Oeste commemorate the newly independent countries – even today these are sneered at by some on the right. The most significant statues are those of **General Jose de San Martin** (national hero of Argentina, Chile and Peru) and **Simón Bolívar** (Venezuelan military leader who liberated Colombia, Venezuela, Ecuador, Peru, Panama and Bolivia from the clutches of the Spanish Empire between 1810 and 1825). The statues in the more prominent Parque de El Retiro are relatively quiet on

Equestrian statue of Simón Bolívar in Parque del Oeste.

the matter of revolutionary heroes – although many of its promenades are named after Latin American countries.

The War of Spanish Succession

Upon the death of the childless Charles II in 1700, an almighty dispute over Spanish succession broke out in Europe. Charles had willed the Spanish crown to the Duke d'Anjou – no less the grandson of Louis XIV of France and his wife Maria Theresa of Austria (i.e., the sister of Charles II). The implications of a combined Spanish and French union were a huge threat for the balance of power in Europe. Accordingly, England, Holland and the Holy Roman Empire formed the core of a 'Grand Alliance' taking on France and Spain. The alliance favoured the Austrian Archduke Charles as successor to the Spanish crown.

After fourteen years of conflict, the Duke d'Anjou was accepted as Spain's king and Austria gave up any rights of succession. However, the Treaty of Utrecht (that formalised the peace between 1713–1715) forced several concessions. These were that Spain and France would not form a union, Spain would cede Naples to Austria and renounce any Flemish inheritance and that Spain would cede Menorca and Gibraltar to Britain, the later regarded today as a '300-year bad joke' in the minds of many Madrileños!

The War of Independence

Having invested heavily in the fleet lost at Trafalgar, due to errors by the French Admiral Villeneuve and an instruction to 'never surrender to superior forces without reaching glory in brave resistance', Spain was financially broke.

In 1807, French forces were invited into Spain in order that Napoleon could attack Britain's ally Portugal, Spain hoping to bag a piece of Portugal in the process. It turned out to be a grave error, as France declared its intention of occupying Spain permanently. Spain, having exhausted its finances on building a fleet to take on Britain, was unable to defend itself in the field – relying on Britain, Portugal and her own meagre army to engage France in the so-called ensuing Peninsular Wars.

Seeing the writing on the wall, Spain's King Ferdinand VII fled Madrid and went into exile, forever damaging the prestige and authority of the Spanish crown. Brazenly, Napoleon appointed his slightly older brother, Joseph Bonaparte, as the new king of Spain. The war lasted six years and affected all parts of the country. Some Spanish hoped for a French-style republic and democracy and encouragingly Joseph Bonaparte adopted some enlightened principles, learned the language and made progressive changes – such as ending the Spanish Inquisition, reintroducing bullfighting and reopening many bars –

although most Spaniards regarded the invader as 'Joe the bottle' for this last act.

Napoleon's forces entered Madrid on 2 May 1808 and were met by a brave uprising of citizens throughout the city, which was the catalyst for the ensuing Peninsular Wars. The largest resistance was in Puerta del Sol, where 'armed with crude weapons' the rebels were quickly defeated by the professional French forces. A plaque outside the headquarters of the Comunidad de Madrid (i.e., the regional government as distinct from city-wide administration based at Cibeles Palace) commemorates the date. The uprising failed and Madrileño rebels were rounded up and executed the following day on **La Montana del Príncipe Pío** in the west of the city (also the location of a massacre during the Civil War in 1936). Goya depicted the uprising and executions in his painting *The Second of May 1808* and *The Third of May 1808* – both hanging in the Museo Nacional del Prado.

French forces suffered their first major defeat of the Peninsular Wars in 1812, when British, Portuguese and

View of Palacio Real from La Montana del Principe Pio.

Spanish forces defeated them at the Battle of Salamanca. And two years later, Spain regained its independence.

During the war, many provinces in Spain attempted to establish independent arrangements for government. Under attack by the French and lacking funds, they established a national government in Cadiz and hosted an inaugural session of the new Spanish Cortes in September 1810. The Cortes ratified 'The Constitution of 1812', proclaiming allegiance to the king and progressive principles like freedom of expression, free press, a national education system and primary schools for every town.

Abolishing the financial and political privileges of the rich, the 1812 Constitution was short-lived. Once the War of Independence was won in 1814, Ferdinand VII, on returning to the throne, re-imposed his own authority, repealed all progressive laws and imposed absolute monarchical rule. There were repeated rallies against the absolutist monarch, each put down and the protagonists punished. One of the most notable is depicted in a moving painting by Gisbert, *Execution of Torrijos and his companions on the Beach at Malaga*, now in the Prado.

A stately obelisk memorial to the memory of those who died at the hands of Napoleonic troops in May 1808 stands at the **Plaza de la Lealtad** on Paseo del Prado. The **Monumento a los Caidos por Espana** (Monument to the Fallen for Spain) contains the ashes of many of the dead in an urn at its base. A further monument, depicting the dramatic events, is situated near Mount Principe Pio, on the south side of Plaza de Espana. Remembering the date, 2 May, is a local holiday in Madrid.

Local eats

Viena Capellanes (C. de Ruiz de Alarcon) is one of a chain of restaurants throughout Madrid. It's known for its 'menu del dia' consisting of healthy and tasty Spanish classics served over two courses (i.e., primeros y segundos) – e.g., gazpacho to start and dishes based around eggs, ham, cod, lamb, tuna, chicken, beef and fresh vegetables. Much recommended and assisted here by its obscure basement entrance, it is off the tourist radar, despite being less than 200 metres from the Prado.

In the district of Malasana, named after a young seamstress who was executed by the French for protecting her honour with a pair of scissors, is the **Plaza del Dos de Mayo**. It commemorates the two soldiers who led the insurgency against the invaders by attacking the Monteleon barracks and capturing arms on 2 May 1808. Today, the plaza is a vibrant place with numerous bars and restaurants.

Plaza de la Lealtad.

Local eats

Locally, a must-visit trio of bars and eateries starts with Madrid's most lively vermouth (i.e., vermut, pronounced 'bermu') bar, **Casa Camacho** (C. de San Andres), followed by further imbibing over a board game at **La Manuela** (C. de San Vicente Ferrer), an institution reminiscent of a Parisian brasserie, and ending with a traditional Spanish meal at **Casa Macareno** (C. de San Vicente Ferrer), loved by many locals and visitors for its humming atmosphere, traditional feel and fine *al la carte* specials (such as pig's cheeks).

Statue of Daoiz and Velarde, Plaza del Dos de Mayo.

Casa Camacho.

La Manuela.

Opposite the Cibeles Fountain stands the current-day headquarters of the Spanish Army. It was formerly the **Palacio de Buenavista** and residence of the Duke of Alba before the family seat moved to the Palacio de Liria.

Local eats

Boasting 62 grape varieties and 125 Spanish wines from 72 regions, **Vinoteca Vides** (C. de la Libertad) is cherished territory for pilgrims seeking vinos Espanols, accompanied by Spanish cheeses. Just don't ask for Albarino – not to the liking of the founder and former television personality Vicente Herrero.

The Spanish Civil War and Siege of Madrid

It seemed that a military coup was inevitable – the question was from which end of the political spectrum it would spring. Through 1936, the army watched on as violence and social chaos consumed the country – biding its time until the conditions were judged right. Making matters worse were well-founded concerns of a Communist revolution and bizarre (unfounded) fears of a worldwide Jewish conspiracy.

The gun for the coup was finally cocked over two days in July 1936. On 12 July, a young socialist in the Government's Assault Guard, Jose Castillo, was murdered by a Falangist gang. The following day the charismatic right-wing politician and monarchist Claudio Sotelo was kidnapped and murdered in retribution for Castillo's death – serious enough, but worsened by the evidence that members of the Assault Guard committed the kidnapping.

The double killing triggered the long-planned military coup of a cabal of generals led by the passionate Emilio Mola and the calculating Francisco Franco. It failed in its immediate objectives and the country split between rebel (i.e., Nationalist) forces occupying large parts of the north and mostly rural west – and Government (i.e., Republican) forces occupying the centre, south and mostly urban east of the country. The war would rage for three years and claim half a million deaths.

At 5 am on 18 July 1936, General Mola gave the order for the uprising. Mola worked down from the north and Franco worked up from the south, having been airlifted into Andalucia along with the Spanish Moroccan Army with assistance from the German and Italian air forces. As George Orwell wrote: 'Franco's rising was a military mutiny backed up by the aristocracy and the Church – an attempt not so much to impose Fascism but restore Feudalism.'

Despite being up against well-trained Nationalist and Africanistas troops equipped with German and Italian arms, munitions and tanks, the Republican Army, assault guards, various armed militias and worker unions repelled the uprising. As landowners sided with the rebels, some parts of central Spain were lost, with consequences for food supply – but the Republicans controlled the large cities and ports, principally: Madrid, Barcelona, Valencia, Bilbao and Malaga.

In Madrid, a tragic and early confrontation was the siege at the Government's Montana barracks in Principe Pio over 18–20 July 1936. The allegiance of troops to the Republican cause was uncertain and after two attempts to offer clemency to those inside (who were not united in their thinking), a combined force of 8,000 militia and assault guards attacked the barracks, resulting in a grim massacre of hundreds of troops. The Montana Barracks is remembered today with a large frieze at its former site, now home to the Temple of Debod.

The coup progressed to a brutal Civil War that would last until the fall of Madrid on 28 March 1939. Germany and Italy funded the rebels, whilst Russia and Portugal supported the Republican Government. The British and French stayed neutral, preferring to see a Nationalist victory than side with Russia and risk losing Spain to the communists. The concept of a communist state adjacent to Gibraltar, with its strategic control of the Mediterranean, was unthinkable for the Conservative Government of Stanley Baldwin. Behind the scenes, the financial centre of the City of London funded aspects of the Nationalist cause whilst Texaco supplied it with oil – as Peter Day describes in detail in *Franco's Friends.*

Mola died in an air crash in mid-1937 and Franco took overall control of the Nationalist forces, pursuing his brutal agenda to preserve the old economic order, protect Catholicism, prevent communism and guard against the bizarre threat of world Jewry. Franco started out a mild-mannered child intending on a naval career, cut short by the destruction of the Spanish Navy by the United States and loss of its colonies in 1898. He joined army school and despite bullying for his precociousness, progressed rapidly, proving his ability as a leader in Africa. Obsessed with promotion, he was quickly made a major and went on to become the youngest general in the Spanish Army, commanding the Spanish Foreign Legion. Under his political sponsor, Miguel Primo de Rivera, he displayed ruthlessness in 1921 in the hills of Asturias, brutally putting down a miners' strike. He despised the Republican Government that posted him out of the way to a command in the Canary Islands in 1936.

Franco attempted an immediate capture of Madrid by attacking from the west, which failed. Fortune favoured the capital by two factors; battle plans found on a dead Italian officer forewarned Republican forces of the location of the attack and the Italian supplied Fiat light tanks were no match for the steep terrain in **Parque del Oeste**. Today, the park is a favourite of Madrileños for its mature plantings, challenging running routes, rose garden and sculptures – all in sharp contrast to the devastation it suffered during the war, to which there are several reminders *in situ*. With too many battlefronts throughout Spain, Franco withdrew forces from Madrid in mid-November 1936 and Parque del Oeste became the front line of a three-year siege of Madrid. Running south alongside the park to the Templo of Debod, Paseo de Pintor Rosales offers views west to the Casa de Campo.

Local eats

There are numerous bars and restaurants along what is now, arguably, Madrid's most beautiful boulevard. **Marcelino Vinos** (C. del Pintor Rosales) is a buzzing bar with extensive roadside seating.

Intent on beating the city into submission, Franco pursued a campaign of aerial bombing and daily artillery

Pillbox. Parque del Oeste.

Marcelino Vinos.

shelling from the Casa de Campo in the west, preferring to 'destroy Madrid than leave it to the Marxists'. A key target was Madrid's tallest building (and Europe's first skyscraper), the **Edificio Telefonica** on Gran Via. Built in 1930, and hit over one hundred times during the war, it served not only as a telephone exchange but also an observation post for Francoist movements outside the city. Today, it hosts four floors of exhibitions on topics of media and technology. Salamanca district, with its wealthy, right-leaning residents, was spared the bombing and shelling.

Local eats

La Terraza de Oscar (Hotel Room Mate Oscar, Pl. de Pedro Zerolo) is a spacious roof terrace with excellent views of Madrid. Its unadvertised presence makes it lesser known; just enter the hotel and ask to visit the terrace. One of Madrid's most authentic dining experiences is at **La Tasca Suprema** (C. de Argensola), where fine food complemented by lively groups

Edificio Telefonica.

La Tasca Suprema.

of Madrileños makes the occasion indelible.

Franco's murder of thousands of civilians in nearby Badajoz led to a climate of terror in Madrid. Guards, militias and civilians reciprocated with atrocities throughout the city visited on suspected rebel Nationalists (i.e., the Fifth Column). One of the worst atrocities was the murder of Nationalist prisoners in the Modelo Prison in Moncloa, following an incompetent move of inmates to a more secure prison outside of Madrid. Today the site is occupied by the authoritarian-looking **General Headquarters of the Air and Space Force**.

Local eats

Cerveceria **Argos Restaurante** (C. de Hilarion Eslava) is a local institution catering to all ages and showing sports on three large screens.

General Headquarters of the Air and Space Force, from Faro de Moncloa.

All seated diners, young and old, display their feelings on the live football or bull fighting programmes. It is a good place to share a plate of Huevos Rotos.

Madrileños bravely put up with the bombardments, the city bedecked with banners declaring 'No Pasaran' (They shall not pass). The siege lasted until the end of the war.

In 1936, the Republican Government commissioned Pablo Picasso to paint a scene that epitomised the horror being visited upon Spain by the Nationalists. He depicted dramatic images of the bombing of Madrid and Malaga (his home town). Before it was displayed at the 1937 World's Fair in Paris, a journalist suggested naming the work *Guernica* – the northern town that had suffered indiscriminate bombing by German aircraft. Today, *Guernica* attracts thousands to see it hanging upstairs in the Museo Nacional Centro de Arte Reina Sofía, along with other paintings and posters from the Civil War and a world-renowned collection of mainly twentieth century art.

Division in the Republican Government, comprising a fragile coalition of socialists, communists and anarchists (named the Popular Front), made central control of war efforts by its progressive leader (Francisco Caballero) challenging and lacking in trust. George Orwell spoke of the absence of modern arms in Catalonia – possibly for fear of anarchist uprisings by the Republican centre. In May 1937, Caballero gave way to Juan Negrin, who remained prime minister until the defeat of the Government. Negrin relied heavily on communist support and arms from Russia to fuel the war – a fact that alienated him from the socialists and liberals in the party. President of the Republic, Manuel Azana, failed to remove Negrin via a coup – the fact that Azana was in exile did not help the cause.

The Nationalists styled themselves defenders of the faith – and with 13 bishops and up to 7,000 clergy killed in the first few months of the war, the church was only too glad to have the protection of Franco's army, making the Civil War a Catholic crusade with the approval of the Church in Rome.

International Brigades of volunteers (such as George Orwell, Jack Jones and Laurie Lee from the UK, and Ernest Hemingway from the USA) joined the Republican cause. Russia and Stalin mainly funded the brigades. All Republican forces were termed the 'Reds' by the Nationalists.

As four army columns moved toward Madrid, Franco leveraged his partnership with the Falange Party for political support and intelligence from militant sympathisers in the city – it was his so-called Fifth Column.

As World War II loomed, Russian support for the Spanish government waned and later was withdrawn. Having exhausted the country's gold reserves, estimated at around 500 tons, for arms (many blocked at the French/Spanish border due to the policy of non-intervention) and with no funds or foreign backers remaining, the Spanish Republic's days were numbered. From July–November 1938, the Battle of the Ebro raged in Catalonia. Starved of decent equipment the Republicans lost to the Nationalists and 70,000 lives were sacrificed. In the end, according to estimates by Paul Preston in *The Spanish Civil War*, deaths were around 500,000 across both sides, out of a population of 25 million. Preston estimates 300,000 losses on the battlefield and 200,000 civilian losses (three quarters of which were in the Franco zone). This excludes subsequent deaths of refugees and prisoners who later died in captivity. In short, Preston maintains that the Republicans lost the war because Britain and France stayed away.

On 28 March 1939, Franco's massed armies moved on Madrid, virtually unopposed. And on 1 April, General Franco announced the end of fighting. For nearly 40 years, Spain would become a totalitarian state under a military dictatorship – with Franco as Head of State and Government, going by the title El Caudillo (i.e., the military and political leader). George Orwell wrote, 'that a political climate in which western powers were anxious to appease the Fascist Axis and preferred a pro-Franco Spain to a probably pro-Russian one, left the Spanish Republic with no hope of survival'.

Today, there are very few memorials to the Second Republic – many were systematically removed by the Franco regime. But like a ghost of the past, the **Cabestreros Fountain** in the district of Lavapies still stands, proclaiming *Republica Espanola, 1934*.

Local eats

Nearby **La Taberna Antonio Sanchez** (C. del Meson de Paredes) is one of Madrid's best preserved nineteenth-century bars, with resplendent tile work and a zinc bar. **Café Barbieri**

Cabestreros Fountain.

La Corrala de Tribulete.

Café Barbieri Restaurante.

La Taberna Antonio Sanchez.

Restaurante (C. del Ave Maria) is an impressive, mirrored, turn of the twentieth century, café for coffees and Italian-themed food – pizzas being the speciality. Located in Lavapies, one of the fast-disappearing gritty neighbourhoods, the bohemian feel contrasts with other neighbourhoods.

At the more modest end of the lifestyle spectrum, **La Corrala de Tribulete** (Mesón de Paredes) is an example of an 1882 corridor tenement in the nearby working-class (but fast gentrifying) area of Embajadores – a must-see location for street art.

Arco de Moncloa (formerly Arco de la Victoria) was built under orders from Francisco Franco to commemorate victory in the Civil War in 1955. Standing at 40 metres in a prominent position for traffic approaching Madrid from the west, it's a triumphal gate at what was the front line of the Civil War. At the top, a sculpture of Minerva, the Greek goddess of war, drives a chariot. Nearby is the earlier circular monument to the Fallen from Madrid, with a cupola. These are somewhat awkward sights, apparently celebrating the outcome of the Civil War. Successive governments and authorities have adopted a 'leave it alone' policy, not wishing to rule on the future of these controversial buildings.

Local eats

Heladeria Los Alpes (C. Arcipreste de Hita) is recognised as Madrid's oldest Italian ice-cream shop. Established in 1950, it serves artisanal ice-cream and cakes in a refreshingly authentic-style parlour.

Arco de Moncloa from Faro de Moncloa.

Casa de Campo is around three kilometres west of the city centre of Madrid. An enormous rural park, it is twice the size of London's Richmond Park. Originally a royal hunting ground established by Philip II, and retained by subsequent royals until the Second Republic finally opened it to the public in 1933, it's a favourite weekend retreat of Madrileños. At its centre, the hill Cerro de Garabitas (675m) commands a strategic position over Madrid – a feature used by Franco's Nationalist forces to shell the city during the Civil War. Military bunkers still dot the landscape. Aside from the running, cycling and hiking, add an outdoor swimming complex, a theme park, a zoo and a boating lake surrounded by restaurants. You will need a few Sunday visits to exhaust the recreational opportunities.

Local eats

El Urogallo (Casa de Campo) is one of several lakeside cafés that serve food and drinks all day, including generous proportions of fine dining – table-top steak grills make for a voluminous and fun occasion. Excellent for pre-booked large parties and families, the sunsets over the lake also make it a vivid memory.

Casa de Campo.

Lago, Casa de Campo.

El Urogallo.

BELIEF AND PRAYER

The Catholic monarchs

Modern Spain was established with the marriage of Isabella I of Castile and Ferdinand II of Aragon (father of Catherine of Aragon) in 1479 – operating as one crown with two kingdoms, like Scotland and England (between 1603 and 1707). Of the other principal kingdoms in the north of the Iberian Peninsula, Leon had reunified with Castile in 1301 with Navarre being incorporated in 1512, whilst Portugal had become an independent country in 1143. Today the coat of arms at the centre of the flag of Spain denotes the founding kingdoms; displaying the castle of Castile, lion of Leon, red and gold stripes of Aragon, golden chains of Navarre and the pomegranate of the Emirate of Granada, conquered in 1492.

The legacy of Isabella I and Ferdinand II runs deep in the psyche of many in modern Spain. The struggle that brought the reunification of the country was promulgated under their rule. Today, these Catholic Monarchs are revered by church and state alike – many on the right appealing to their memory to maintain a unified Spain and to not permit any fragmentation that regional independence (e.g., in Catalonia or the Basque Country) would produce.

The Christian Monarchs were enthusiastic empire builders – offering conquered lands to subjects that promised to develop and defend the territory in their name. This policy, one of the first of its kind in Europe, accelerated emigration and gave a taste of freedom to those involved, escaping the feudal conditions still prominent throughout Europe. The Monarchs were also among the first to set up the policies, infrastructure and practices of statecraft, maintaining and developing possessions in the Americas and the Mediterranean (i.e., Italy) supported by a cadre of civil servants and diplomats.

The Empire's prospects were further assured by the marriage of Joanna (daughter of the Catholic Monarchs) and Philip I (son of Maximillian I, the Holy Roman Emperor and Mary of Burgundy). The marital union heralded the pre-eminence of the Habsburg Empire, ruling throughout Spain, Austria, Netherlands and parts of Italy – an empire whose leaders

Casa y torre de los Lujanes.

would sit at the top table of European geopolitics until its collapse at the end of World War I, having been unable to extricate itself from a military alliance with Germany.

Madrid during this period was a backwater rarely visited by the monarchs, considered 'a mountain city with a mountain climate' long before Ernest Hemingway described it as such. There are few sights of this time around today, but some contemporary buildings remain – principally the **Casa y torre de los Lujanes** (of the noble Lujanes family) – Madrid's oldest medieval house in Plaza de la Villa and dating from the late 1400s. The architecture is typical of the Mudejar style, blending Christian (i.e., the house, casa) and Muslim (i.e., the tower, torre) elements.

Madrid's oldest church, San Nicolas de Bari de los Servitas, also dates from the 1400s and possibly earlier (see later).

The Spanish Inquisition

Intent on achieving Christian purity throughout Spain, the Catholic Monarchs attempted to convert non-Christians to Christianity. Jews that agreed to be converted to Christianity were known as Conversos, whilst converted Muslims were known as Moriscos. Conversion would bestow the rights and privileges of being a Christian. Those who declined would be denied these rights but could still live peacefully among other citizens in Madrid. By 1480, the thinking had hardened and all non-Christians were forced to either convert to Christianity – or live outside of the city walls.

In 1492, after the reconquest, a cleric named Torquemada persuaded the Catholic Monarchs that there was a risk of insurrection by non-Christians. Heeding his fears, the Catholic Monarchs decided that all non-Christians and Moriscos should be expelled from Spain. Conversos could however remain. It was a policy that resulted in a mass exodus of around three million Moors and Jews over the period between 1492 and 1610 and a depletion of culture, resources and revenue – not a smart move in this febrile period of European geopolitics.

To prevent lip-service being paid to Christianity, the converted Jews that remained (i.e., Conversos) could be examined under the notorious Spanish Inquisition, a programme that would last from 1492 to 1834. The Spanish Inquisition took its roots from Roman courts and later by the Catholic Church, where the emphasis was on getting at the truth via questions. The intention was to identify insincere Christians (i.e., those Jews who had converted to Christianity to access privileges but were still practicing Judaism). Those who hid their true faith were penalised and given the option of either being expelled or having a second chance to truly adopt Christianity and desist from non-Christian worship. Second offenders, and those who lied or chose martyrdom, would be burned (purifying their soul) – only being first garrotted if they recanted their 'sins'. It is estimated that around 100,000 were prosecuted by the Inquisition, of which 3–5 per cent were killed.

Plaza Mayor was the location of the open-air court of the Spanish Inquisition in Madrid. Here the auto-de-fe (i.e., act of faith) was the public ceremony at which accused were judged – and either repented their heresy or were handed over to secular authorities for the sentences to be carried out. Burnings would take place outside of the city walls to avoid the risk of conflagration in the plaza. Plaques in the plaza recall the commissions and these events and the scene is represented in detail in the painting *Auto-da-fe in the Plaza Mayor of Madrid*, by the Spanish painter Francisco Rizi, hanging in the Museo del Prado.

Symbols of faith

Madrid has over eighty churches representing architectural styles from: Mudejar, Gothic, Renaissance, Baroque, Neo-classical and Modern.

Completed in 1785, and hosting Spain's largest dome, the **Basilica de San Francisco El Grande** is a breath-taking example of the neo-classical style architecture, completed by Francesco Sabatini, the versatile architect of San Carlos Hospital (now the Museo Reina Sofia), Alcala Gate and Madrid's sewage system in the late 1700s. Like many other large buildings in conflict-torn Madrid, it also functioned as a barracks in the mid-1800s during the Carlist Wars. According to legend, the church stands on land offered to St Francis of Assisi in 1214 and hosts a collection of paintings including works by Goya and Zurbaran as well as prominent statues of important saints.

Local eats

El Camarote (Pl. de Puerta de Moros) is a bustling tapas bar and an attractive first-floor family restaurant serving typical Spanish dishes.

South of Plaza Mayor, *en route* to the famous Sunday Rastro Market, **La Real Congregacion de San Isidro de Madrid** towers over the Calle de Toledo. Not only is San Isidro (a labourer/farmer in Madrid in the 1100s) the patron saint of Madrid and the church his place of

Basilica de San Francisco El Grande from La Latina.

burial, but it was Madrid's unofficial cathedral before La Almudena was consecrated in 1993. Some of the church dates from the mid-1600s whilst the impressive baroque edifice (designed by Ventura Rodriguez) was constructed in the 1760s. It fell victim to anti-religious fervour at the start of the Spanish Civil War causing widespread damage and collapse of the dome, now painstakingly restored and richly decorated.

Local eats

Opposite the church, **Cafeteria Taberna San Bruno** (C. de Toledo) serves traditional tapas and raciones around a square bar, also providing an extensive weekend menu, either dining inside or on the terrace.

Madrid's oldest church is **San Nicolas de Bari de los Servitas**. It's another religious building damaged during the Civil War and restored and declared a national monument in 1947. The site dates to the early 1200s, but it may have housed a mosque prior to that date. The current building is from 1650 and consists of Muslim and Christian architectural styles – proving that Mudejar architecture remained popular long after Muslims were expelled. The square tower is typical Mudejar style whilst the central apse is gothic. Juan de Herrera, favourite architect of Philip II and responsible for the world-famous El Escorial Palace, was originally buried in the church.

La Real Congregacion de San Isidro de Madrid.

Cafeteria Taberna San Bruno.

Local eats

Nearby **El Butillin** (Pl. de Santiago) is an ideal spot for coffees, snacks and casual dining. The terrace is in a safe, traffic-free location for families with young children.

The **Iglesia Parroquial de San Jerónimo el Real** – or simply, Los Jerónimo's – has an illustrious past dating to when the site was granted religious orders by Queen Isabella I. The monastery was home to the swearing-in of subsequent monarchs as Princes/Princesses of Asturias – a title granted to the heir apparent of the Spanish crown, currently held by Princess Leonor. The impressive gothic building dates from the mid-1500s with later additions, most notably the entrance staircase, built for the wedding of King Alfonso XIII and Victoria Eugenie (Queen Victoria's granddaughter) in 1906. With such royal connections, today it takes the mantle of being Madrid's society church. It is believed that the square tower of the church may have initially been the minaret of a mosque before it was later consecrated as a catholic church, another example of the Mudejar style (i.e., built by Muslims under Christian rule).

San Nicolas de Bari de los Servitas.

Local eats

Opposite Los Jerónimo's, **Caixa Forum** hosts a cultural and arts centre and exhibition spaces. Originally a power station, the building, appearing to float above the ground, opened in 2008. Its fourth-floor bar and restaurant is a good place to eat or just have a coffee overlooking the Museo del Prado and Real Jardin Botanico.

Away from central Madrid one can view original frescoes by Francisco de Goya in **San Antonio de la Florida Chapel** – and pay respects at his tomb (although the artist's head is missing, the source of national mystery!). The frescoes celebrate a miracle of Saint Antony of Padua, one of Madrid's most popular saints, owing to his association

Iglesia Parroquial de San Jerónimo el Real.

CaixaForum.

with bringing lovers together in matrimony (celebrated every June 13th). The chapel was declared a national monument in 1905 and in 1928 an identical place of worship was built adjacent to the original chapel to provide a home for the congregation and religious service, preserving Goya's masterpieces *in situ*.

Local eats

A stone's throw from the chapel, **Casa Mingo** (Paseo de la Florida) is a large bar and restaurant famed for its roast chicken and cider.

The **Monasterio de las Descalzas Reales** is frequently dubbed the most aristocratic of Madrid's convents owing to it being the residence of the monarch on visits to the city before the construction of the Palacio Real, many disliking the spartan conditions of the medieval Alcazar. The monastery was established in 1559 by Maria of Austria (daughter of Charles V) and the original sisters were drawn from noble or

San Antonio de la Florida Chapel.

aristocratic families. Today, it is home to around 20 Franciscan nuns, who still don open-toed sandals all year round. The daily tours show off the interior, resplendent with religious imagery and spiritual icons, plus works by Goya and Bruegel.

Local eats

Valdemeso (C. de Mesonero Romanos) is a busy locals' and workers' bar, offering complimentary tapas (often a small dish of paella) with drinks. It also has a basic restaurant serving a range of dishes from the 'menu del dia'.

Nearby in Calle del Codo, one can experience an altogether lighter aspect of the sisterhood of the **Convento de las Carboneras**. Most days, home-made sweets and biscuits are available for purchase via a peculiar swinging turntable, enabling the nuns of this closed monastery to be heard – but not seen.

Local eats

Federal Café (Pl. de las Comendadoras) is a good choice for European and American style brunches and (during weekdays

Monasterio de las Descalzas Reales.

Federal Cafe.

Catedral de la Almudena.

only) an excellent work-café. An equally good sister-location is in Pl. de las Comendadoras, packed with researchers and humming with silent-commerce. Also locally, **Tablao Las Carboneras** (C. del Conde de Miranda) is one of Madrid's best Flamenco bars, with shows starting around 11pm.

After years of unsuccessful petitioning to the Archdiocese of Toledo that Madrid should be permitted its own bishopric, Pope Leo XIII intervened in 1885 to make it so. After years of interrupted construction, Pope John Paul II finally consecrated the **Catedral de la Almudena** (i.e., cathedral of the city) (C. de Bailen) in 1993. Known simply as La Almudena, it is built on the site of a former Muslim mosque. Original plans by Franciso de Cuba in 1879 and many subsequent redesigns have resulted in a 'hotch-potch of gothic revival and baroque', in the opinion of the writer Jules Stewart. Its construction was funded mainly out of bequests from wealthy aristocrats – a fact that sits uneasily with many Madrileños today. The cathedral does however host several modern friezes and works of art, both beautiful and unusual in the setting. The crypt houses a medieval statue of the Virgin Mary (Virgen de la Almudena) and an image of San Isidro – both patron saints of Madrid. Nearby, stands a more recent bronze statue of **El Vecino Curioso,** the Curious Neighbour, (C. de la Almudena) peering into the archaeological remains of an earlier church that stood before the cathedral. This memorial is much less formal – the worn brass signifying that a pinch on his bottom may bring good luck!

Catedral de la Almudena.

Near the Palacio Real, the **Monasterio de la Encarnacion** was founded in 1611 by the wife of Philip III, Magaret of Austria. Another building by court favourite Juan Gomez de Mora, it represents the baroque style. A closed convent of cloistered Augustinian nuns, it is replete with key religious works and is home to the treasured relic of Saint Pantaleón.

Local eats

Operating since 1870, the dining room of **La Bola** (C. de la Bola) imbues one with traditional Castilian culture and cuisine. Renowned for the best El Cocido Madrileño in the city.

Monasterio de la Encarnacion.

THE HABSBURGS

Father and son

In 1500, the union between Joanna and Philip I that enlarged the Austrian Habsburg Empire to include Spain, produced a son. In 1516, he became Charles I of Spain and three years later, upon the death of his grandfather, inherited the title of Charles V Holy Roman Emperor. Charles I abdicated in 1556 and his son became Philip II of Spain whilst Charles' brother, Ferdinand I, inherited the title Holy Roman Emperor. Marriage and birth consolidated the Habsburg, Burgundian, Aragon and Castilian dynasties into the most powerful empire the world had seen.

From the start, Charles I put his energies into empire building, adding vast territories in the Americas and the Pacific, making it an empire where the sun never set. Philip II followed his father's lead, adding trade routes, taking on the Ottomans in the Mediterranean, pursuing religious wars with the French and combatting the naval incursions of Protestant England and the Netherlands – partly religious conflict and wholly about trade.

Madrid was a stopover for the itinerant court of Charles I, known for its pure water and flour mills – making it a centre of bread production. The Moorish Alcazar perched on an escarpment facing west made it an interesting place and it was developed by both Charles I and Philip II using their favoured architects (e.g., Juan Bautista de Toledo, Juan de Herrera, Francisco de Mora and Juan Gomez de Mora), adding artworks now housed in the Prado. It was connected to the Real Monasterio de la Encarnacion via an elevated pathway. A fabulous scale model of the precinct (and many other related artefacts) can be seen at the Museo de Historia de Madrid. Furthermore, a three-dimensional map of Madrid is at the Museo de San Isidro. This displays the evolution of Madrid and its city gates from the original Alcazar in the 800s, the Medina (added in the 900s), Christian conquest and expansion in the 1100s, suburban growth through the 1200–1400s and the enlarged city of Philip II undertaken during his reign (1556–1598).

The Empire was managed as a set of unconnected territories, lacking any central organisational infrastructure and managed personally by the king and his closest advisers. Charles' advice to Philip was not to depend too much on one person, so finding himself unable to delegate he drowned in administrative detail, no doubt impairing his ability to see the imperial wood from its trees.

Philip II was so taken with Madrid that he made it the country's capital in 1561. The itinerant court ceased and it became Philip's permanent seat of power. It is not recorded why Madrid was selected over other candidates, like Toledo, Valladolid or Salamanca. Attractive reasons could have been: to escape ecclesiastical oversight in Toledo, to occupy a defensive location, to avoid the aristocracy in Valladolid, the drier air would have helped his wife's medical condition, its centrality in the peninsula, a suitable already-built palace ready to be modernised (i.e., the Alcazar), there were good hunting grounds nearby and it was close to the mausoleum he had built to the memory of his father at El Real Monasterio de San Lorenzo de El Escorial. Or simply, like Madrid's name means in Arabic – it was 'the place of many springs'.

Despite Madrid's elevation, it was surrounded by woodlands protecting it from the elements coming down from the Guadarrama mountains – but sadly, for future generations, these woods were chopped down before their shielding value was understood. During the harsher months Philip would vacate to lush Aranjuez, the cooler north near Oviedo, or El Escorial – or more locally to the Palacio Real de El Pardo.

On becoming the capital, Madrid immediately attracted aristocrats, nobles, clerics, government officials, intellectuals, artists and artisans – all seeking advancement and influence with the king and his court. Practically overnight the population swelled by around 14,000 people – causing a housing crisis, dealt with by a decree forcing shared use of dwellings, leading to a whole sub-culture of obfuscation.

With the Dutch and Portuguese Wars of Independence raging, Philip set about modernizing the city. Backing off east of the Alcazar's escarpment, the Casa de Campo was built as an enormous royal hunting ground (finally opened to the public in 1931). Lacking planning, residential development was mostly haphazard except for Plaza Mayor – replacing the original Plaza del Arrabal and bringing the main square inside the city walls (for the purposes of taxation). Madrid was declared the capital city during the middle of Spain's Golden Age. It would go on to attract the great artists of the period like Diego Velazquez, Miguel de Cervantes and Francisco de Quevedo, settling in El Barrio de las Letras. The old roads (being the main arteries) were Alcalá Street (west to Guadalajara), Atocha (east to Valencia), Toledo (south road to Andalusia) and Segovia (north road to Extremadura). The predominant style of architecture among the rich was distinctly Austrian Habsburg – easily identified today by black-slatted pitched roofs and corner turrets – one of the best examples being the Casa de la Villa in the Plaza de la Villa.

The centre of Madrid's commercial and municipal life during the reigns of Charles I and Philip II was the **Plaza de la Villa**. Originally an Arab street market, it was an important place to be when Madrid was the capital of the world's largest empire. It is home to some of the most historic buildings in Madrid – the oldest being the palace of a knight's family: Casa y Torre de Lujanes. The tower may have been home to King Francis I of France, held captive after the Battle of Pavia in Italy in 1525.

The baroque **Casa de la Villa** on its western side is the work mainly of Juan Gomez de Mora. Constructed in 1640 in typically Austrian style, it was home to Madrid's City Council from 1693 to 2007 – before municipal offices moved to the Palacio de Cibeles in the west of Madrid. It's steeply sloping

Plaza de la Villa.

Monument to citizens transported to Nazi concentration camps, 1940-45, Plaza de la Villa.

roof of tiling, designed to let snow slide off easily and coloured black to retain the heat, are useful features in Austrian Habsburg properties, but clearly unnecessary in Madrid. Today, it is still home to various departments of the Ayuntamiento (i.e., municipal council) of Madrid. On its south side the plateresque-style (i.e., richly ornamented) **Casa de Cisneros** was home to the wealthy Cardinal Cisneros and his family from 1537 – today also housing various departments of the Ayuntamiento (i.e., Community) of Madrid. In the centre of the square is the statue of the one-time favourite of Philip II, Admiral Alvaro de Bazan.

Local eats

Taberna La Concha (C. de la Cava Baja), appreciated for its own blend of Vermouth, and **Taberna Tempranillo** (C. de la Cava Baja), a truly castizo restaurant with rustic décor, serving

Casa de la Villa.

Casa de Cisneros.

Madrid cuisine with an extensive list of fine wines.

Madrid's most historic and majestic monument is **Plaza Mayor** – the main square. Conceived by Philip II and his architect Juan Gomez de Mora, its original purpose was to absorb the old Arab market within the city walls (probably for the purposes of taxation). It is a lasting and significant monument to the king. The square was finally inaugurated in 1619, during the early years of Philip III, becoming a popular residential area for members of the Royal Court. Philip III's equestrian statue stands in the centre of the square with one leg of the horse raised, signifying the rider was injured in battle, arguably a moot point. Most of the statue is a replacement of the original destroyed by rioting in 1931. Plaza Mayor has been a scene of royal ceremonies, inquisitions, executions, bull fights and destructive fires – and, crucially, home to the city's historical Casa de Panaderia (i.e., bakery) and Casa de la Carniceria (i.e., butcher) – both ensuring the continuity of food supply.

Today, the oldest building in the plaza is the Casa de Panaderia (now the central tourist office). A devasting bakery fire in the early 1670s spread to the timber buildings in the square. A new stone bakery was viewed prudent, built in 1674, but the residences were still made of timber. History repeated itself 100 years later and the sole survivor of the conflagration was the bakery. The lesson was learned and in 1790 all replacement construction was in stone, the work of Juan de Villanueva. The bakery was adorned with frescoes in the 1990s – making it a beautiful sight for residents of the square and guests of the leading hotel chain opposite (Cristiano Ronaldo's Pestana) occupying the former butcher's.

Local eats

There are numerous bars and restaurants near Plaza Mayor. On Calle de Cuchilleros, **Casa Botin** (C. de Cuchilleros) is the world's oldest restaurant – verified by the Guinness Book of Records. It was established by the Frenchman Monsieur Botin and his nephew (i.e., 'sobrino') in 1725. Goya worked as a kitchen hand at Botin, perhaps helping in the preparation of suckling pig – one of the restaurant's specialities. Pork is historically popular in Spain as pigs do not require grass to graze and eating the meat was a useful test of religious affinity during the Inquisition, against those hiding Judaism.

Next door to Casa Botin, is Europe's oldest barber shop displaying the traditional colours on a pole of red, white and blue, representing the blood, bandages and veins of their original twin role as barber surgeons. Also notice the small bronze plaques outside business premises, signifying the business has

Plaza Mayor.

Statue of Philip III, Plaza Mayor.

paid local taxes for more than 100 years. Prevalent throughout Madrid, it's a form of recognition and thanks to the commercial world.

The stunning **Palacio Real de El Pardo** was built by Charles I and expanded in the 1700s. Located about five miles north of Madrid, it is situated in the Parque El Pardo – a former hunting ground and now a rural expanse for hiking. El Pardo was originally a hunting lodge expanded over the years to a royal residence. The many opulent rooms are filled with paintings, some by Spanish greats like Goya, and tapestries produced at the **Real Fabrica de Tapices** in Madrid. El Pardo was requisitioned by Franco after the Civil War and served as his family residence until he died in 1975. It's a fascinating (if slightly chilling) insight to the dictator's environment during his long years of power, whether you dwell in the Council Room, Franco's office, private cinema or family rooms – all retained as he left them.

Casa Botin.

Palacio Real de El Pardo.

Another city-centre building typical of the seventeenth-century Asturias (i.e., Austrian) architecture (by Juan Gomez de Mora) is the **Palacio de Santa Cruz.** Formerly, it was a jail for members of the Court that had fallen out with the monarch. Since the late 1930s it has been the headquarters of the Ministry of Foreign Affairs.

Taberna Bodegas Ricla.

Local eats
Taberna Bodegas Ricla
(C. de Cuchilleros), a small family-run bar serving small dishes, offering home cooked dishes and a genuine commitment to customer service.

Among Philip II's infrastructure projects is Madrid's oldest bridge, **Segovia Bridge.** Located in the west of Madrid and spanning the River Manzanares flowing down from Segovia, it was declared a Site of Cultural Interest in 1996. Originally started in 1574, the court favourite Juan de Herrera took charge three years later and modernised the medieval designs, making it horizontal. Innovative for the time, this was achieved by using nine semicircular arches. Its width was massively increased after the Civil War and it was improved aesthetically during the creation of Madrid Rio, a riverside fitness and social area opened in 2011.

Local eats
Mercado de Tirso Molina (Calle de Doña Urraca) is well away from the tourist trail, ensuring an authentic experience of drinks, tapas and raciones enhanced by a local vibe, particularly notable on Saturday lunchtime.

North west of Madrid, **San Lorenzo de El Escorial** lunges out of the hill side. A colossal monument to the reign of Philip II, shrine to his father, mausoleum to both father and son and a Royal Palace, it was designed by Juan de Herrera building on a plan by Juan Bautista de Toledo. The artwork has since moved to the Prado, but

San Lorenzo de El Escorial.

Segovia Bridge.

the granite structure moves many to visit the sanctuary that served as Philip's centre of prayer and world campaigning. The Pantheon of Kings, in El Escorial, is the resting place for most of the Spanish monarchs over the last five centuries.

Inept and inbred

After the stellar, albeit aggressive, performance of the father and son act of Charles and Philip, the next hundred years of the Spanish Habsburgs was a story of corruption, depletion and decline – until its eradication altogether in 1700 with the dawn of a new French Bourbon dynasty.

Philip III, the son of Philip II and Anna of Austria, succeeded his father in 1598. His was a more peaceful but unimpressive reign, more taken with hunting. Coming to power nearly halfway through the Dutch Wars of Independence (1568–1648) and possibly recognising the strain on resources, he arranged peace with the other Protestant foe of his father, England, in 1604. And he even encouraged the marriage of his daughter to the English Prince of Wales (later Charles I) in the so-called 'Spanish Match' – a union that failed since the Infanta Maria Anna desired a Catholic partner. Yet, still seized with the need for Christian purity, Philip III expelled all Arabs and Moriscos (i.e., Arabs that had converted to Christianity) in 1609. The infrastructure of Madrid largely stood still during his reign, a time of intense inflation as silver and raw materials flooded into the capital from Spain's colonies in south America.

Philip IV, the son of Philip III and Magaret of Austria, succeeded his father in 1621. He was the most enlightened (and promiscuous) of the Habsburg monarchs – particularly in his love of theatre and mistresses (siring 39 illegitimate, in addition to his 12 legitimate, children). It was on his watch that, despite the success of the Siege of Breda in 1625, the Netherlands gained its independence from Spain in 1648. And Portugal followed in 1668, three years after Philip III's reign ended – the countries becoming twins, joined back-to-back, ever since.

The Spanish fleet had been destroyed by the Dutch in 1639 in the English Channel (at the Battle of the Downs) – ending Spanish naval dominance in the world, and in 1643 the army lost to French forces in the Ardennes (at the Battle of Rocroi). These losses heralded the end of Spanish hegemony in Europe. Even with the sage advice of Count Duke Olivares, the 'Planet King' was a world of shrinking proportions for the Spanish Empire.

With the loss of tax revenues from its former European territories, the Spanish state relied more on national taxation as a means of funding its administration. And Madrid was still a society of masters and servants – more grist to the mill for Nationalists and Separatists.

Charles II, the son of Philip IV and Mariana of Austria, succeeded his father in 1665. He was a physically and mentally sick man, the product of multiple generations of in-breeding among the Habsburgs – a strategy intended to maintain solidarity and succession, but which resulted in Charles being unable to produce an heir. All eight of his grandparents were descended from Joanna (daughter of the Catholic Monarchs). With no heir, the Habsburgs in Spain would cease to exist. The legacy of Philip IV was a ruined country, decaying empire and a sick heir. In Austria, the Habsburg dynasty remained, along with its traditional foe the Ottomans – both dynasties dying out at the end of World War I. In the case of Austria, its leaders were unable to extricate themselves from an alliance with the German Kaiser Wilhelm II.

Inspiring Louis XIV of France to create Versailles, the **Palacio del Buen Retiro** was once a complex of royal buildings, hunting grounds and an enormous formal garden completed in 1635 for the pleasure of Philip IV by his close advisor, the Count Duke of Olivares. Today, only **El Casón del Buen Retiro** (originally the ballroom and now an annex of the Prado) and the **Salon de Reinos** (Hall of Kingdoms), displaying the banners and coats of arms that constituted all the kingdoms of Spain, remain – both buildings projecting Spain's imperial confidence. The rest of the complex was destroyed during the War of Independence. Many of the artworks that were originally displayed in the palacio are hanging in the Prado today. Velazquez imagined *The Surrender of Breda* (c. 1635) for Philip IV. Considered one of the finest historical paintings (and Velazquez's only) of the Spanish Baroque, it depicts one of the major events midway through the Dutch wars of Independence and the religious Thirty Years' War.

Local eats

Mandarin Oriental Ritz Hotel (Pl. de la Lealtad): despite its post-war reputation for refusing admission to 'No tipo Ritz', all are welcome at this venerable hotel from the Belle Epoque. Built in 1910 at the behest of Alfonso XIII to ensure Madrid's parity

Salon de Reinos.

Mandarin Oriental Ritz Hotel.

with London and Paris, top class service can be expected over afternoon tea in the cool, florally rich conservatory.

The **Parque de El Retiro** is the lasting reminder of the original formal garden 'retreat', opened to the public by Charles III in the 1770s. It was entirely re-laid during the nineteenth and early twentieth century following its use as a garrison for Napoleonic troops. Key sights include the **Palacio de Cristal** (1886) and the **Palacio de Velazquez** (1883) – the former is also loved for its lakeside views and turtles. Both buildings are now annexes of the Museo Reina Sofia. In May, La Rosaleda (rose garden) springs into bloom, providing one of the world's best displays. The park is vast, so cycling around it affords the chance to enjoy many more sights such as the boating lake (overlooked by a huge equestrian statue of Alfonso XII), a 400-year-old cypress tree and a statue of Lucifer descending to hell. The statue was highly controversial when it was completed in 1885 – not least because its altitude is 666 metres.

Local eats

Florida Park (Parque de El Retiro) is a bar, restaurant and entertainment venue in the heart of El Retiro, very convenient and a step-change up from the lakeside alternatives at a similar cost.

El Rastro (C. de la Ribera Curtidores) is a highly popular Sunday flea market

Parque de El Retiro.

running downhill from Plaza de Cascorro. It's an historical overflow from Plaza Mayor, when meat was slaughtered at the city's central butcher (i.e., Casa de Carniceria) in the square and transported through Plaza de Tirso de Molina to the market – leaving a trail of blood along the route (i.e., a rastro). Later, the area became a centre of industry, mainly food, pottery and leather goods.

Local eats

Café del Art (Pl. de Cascorro), serving drinks and bakery products, is also one of Madrid's best work-cafés. After the market, head to the nearby **Sala Equis** (C. del Duque de Alba) for live music (from noon on Sunday and 5pm on other days) situated in an old cinema often projecting early black and white silent movies.

Plaza de Oriente, opposite the Palacio Real, is a landscaped garden on the spot where the city was founded during the Arab period. It's little known that it was conceived and built by Joseph Bonaparte in 1811, then enhanced by Isabella II with many statues of Spain's historical kings and queens. These were originally intended to crown the palace but were left at ground level after Isabella had a foreboding their weight would cause the palace to collapse. The plaza is so named because it is located on the eastern side of the palace – facing the Orient. In the middle of the plaza stands a statue of Philip IV by Pietro Tacca in 1621, constructed under guidance from Galileo Galilei. The horse's front legs are hollow, enabling this world-first example of an equestrian statue rearing up on its rear legs.

Velazquez lived and worked near Plaza de Oriente and was reputedly buried in a nearby church. His body has never been discovered, so his memory is marked by a column in the nearby **Plaza de Ramales**.

El Rastro.

Sala Equis.

Local eats

Café de Los Austrias (Pl. de Ramales) is a fine bar and restaurant best experienced on the terrace, with views of the plazas and palace at sunset.

Plaza del Rey is home to the curiously named **Casa de Las Siete Chimeneas** (House of the Seven Chimneys) – apparently each representing one of the seven deadly sins. Designed by architect Antonio Sillero and completed in 1577, it's one of Madrid's oldest buildings, and is now home to the Ministry of Education and Culture. Plenty of lore is associated with the building, not least it was a place of confinement for the illegitimate daughter of Philip II and home of Britain's ambassador to Spain after the Restoration in 1660. The plaza itself is a pleasant refuge off Gran Via served by various cocktail bars and restaurants around its shaded perimeter and a good place to relax around the central fountain.

Equestrian statue of Philip IV, Plaza de Oriente.

Plaza de Ramales.

Local eats

Revoltosa (Pl. del Rey) offers coffees and drinks and, judging by the throughput, padron peppers on a bed of fried breaded calamari is the favourite weekend lunchtime snack.

Right: ***Casa de Las Siete Chimeneas.***

Below: ***Revoltosa.***

Plaza del Rey.

The Siglo de Oro

The Spanish Siglo de Oro (Golden Age) started around the late 1400s and continued through to the late 1600s. Against a background of political unification, geographical expansion and empire building, the themes of religion, humanism and patriotism were explored and tested by creative and brave artists. For the wealthy in Madrid, the main pastimes during this period were religion, intellectual gatherings, afternoon 'paseos', bullfights and theatre. The presence of the royal court attracted artists, writers and thespians to Madrid, soon becoming the nation's leading city for performance. Open air theatres flourished, the Palace de la Zarzuela and the Hall of Comedies at the Alcazar were formative locations. Most successful productions were comedic affairs that portrayed every-day life, often featuring a roguish 'picaresque' character, or satirical comedies, frequently set to music. Making performance accessible all-year-round and less subject to weather conditions, permanent Italian-style theatres were later built. In the late 1500s there were three Royal theatres and three public ones, of which only the Teatro Espanol survives today.

The star writers of the day were feted for their insight, wit and lyrical charm. All born in or near Madrid, they blazed Spain into the premier league of literature.

The first and most famous of these greats is Miguel de Cervantes, author of *Don Quixote de la Mancha*, describing in a satirical style the chivalric exploits of the Don and his low-born companion, Sancho Panza. Written over ten years and published in two parts, it is Spain's most loved piece of literature. Astonishingly, Cervantes and William Shakespeare both died on 23 April 1616 – the two men knowing of each other, but unlikely ever to have met.

Felix Lope de Vega was a prolific playwright, poet and novelist and throughout his more than 1,800 works, he displayed his skill at spinning (comedic) tales of morality that illustrated the frailty of the human condition. An arch-enemy of Cervantes he died in 1635, but his themes, values and subjects were taken up by the successors to his mantle: Tirso de Molina and Pedro Calderon de la Barca.

Initially, Francisco de Quevedo was a successful politician, but after falling afoul of Philip IV he devoted his life to becoming the Spanish master of biting political satire. Using poetry as the vehicle for his wit and satire, he actively criticised all that was unequal or improper in the Spanish court and society. No longer able to put up with his outpourings, Philip IV eventually banished him to monastical house arrest, where he died five years later in 1645.

Tirso de Molina was a theologian and dramatist who applied his vivid imagination to everyday life themes, as displayed in works such as *The Seducer of Seville*. He died in 1648.

It would be some years before Pedro Calderon de la Barca would succeed Lope de Vega as Spain's greatest playwright, attracting audiences to his work, some of which drew on personal experience of his harsh childhood years. Calderon de Barca died in 1681, marking the end of this rich and innovative period, his statue occupying a prominent position in Plaza Santa Ana.

Throughout Madrid, the memory of the city's greats of literature is celebrated. The most popular and impressive sight is the former home of Felix Lope de Vega, the **Casa Museo Lope de Vega**. Situated in the Barrio des Las Letras, the home is decorated and fitted in period art and furnishings, with some of the items having been owned by the writer. The garden is also a peaceful retreat with a small orange grove. Lope de Vega lived here until his death in 1610.

Local eats

Casa González (C. del León) is a bar and restaurant serving alongside its core gourmet store and offering Spanish and local specialities. The two-person window table is the prime location, provided you're comfortable being with the limelight of passers-by.

The **Barrio de Las Letras** was home to all the greats of literature, except for Caldron de Barca. It is a labyrinth of around twenty narrow, atmospheric and historical streets that run downwards from Plaza de Jacinto Benavente to the Prado. Peppered with bars and restaurants, it is one of Madrid's most castizo of districts. **Casa de Cervantes** (C. de Cervantes) is the location where Miguel Cervantes lived and died, marked by an external plaque, with his resting place being in the nearby **Convento de las Trinitarias Descalzas**. Nearby another external

Casa Museo Lope de Vega.

Casa Gonzales.

plaque marks the former home of man-of-the-people, Franciso de Quevedo (C. Lope de Vega).

Local eats

Cervecería Restaurante Quevedo (C. de Quevedo) makes an immediate impression as a welcoming and authentic venue for lunch or tapas at the bar. Despite the high tourist footfall, you are offered a complimentary tapa (of whatever is serving) that can be supplemented with raciones such as the delicious Bacaloa (fried salted cod).

Plaza de Santa Ana is a charming square in the Barrio de Las Letras. Created in 1848 on the plot of a former Habsburg-period convent of the same name, the plaza is surrounded by some famed hostelries. In the square stand two monuments – one to the old master of letters (**Pedro Calderon de la Barca**) and the other to **Federico Garcia Lorca**. Lorca, famed for his intense spiritual poetry and plays, was executed by the Nationalists in the Civil War for his relentless socialist agitation and same-gender attraction. The plaza is also home to Madrid's

Below left: ***Convento de las Trinitarias Descalzas.***

Below right: ***Cervecería Restaurante Quevedo.***

oldest theatre, the Teatro Espanol, and at its west end the modernist 1923 white stone Gran Hotel Reina Victoria (now ME Madrid), once a favourite with bull fighters, towers over the plaza and boasts a roof terrace looking west over the Retiro.

Local eats

Cerveceria Alemana (C. del Príncipe) is a must-visit bar owing to its turn-of-the century design and heritage, being a favourite venue of bull fighters and its associations with Ernest Hemingway (who frequented the bar in the early 1930s to research his non-fiction work *Death in the Afternoon).*

West of the Barrio de Las Letras, **Calle Mayor** runs north along the plaza of the same name. This once royal processional street is the location of the former home of Calderon de Barca (# 61), and the birthplace of Lope de Vega (#50).

Cerveceria Alemana.

Statue of Federico Garcia Lorca, Plaza de Santa Ana.

Local eats

You might find the photographs and live streaming off-putting, but **La Torre del Oro** (Pl. Mayor) is undisputedly the most authentic and accessible of bull-fighting bars in Madrid. You will also notice the price of drinks and paid tapas puts the other restaurants in the plaza firmly in its shadow – just don't peer too closely at the photographs of the bull-inflicted injuries to matadors.

In Plaza Santa Ana, the **Teatro Espanol** staged its first performance in September 1583 and continues to this day – making it the world's oldest theatre with continuous productions. Today's building dates from 1745.

Local eats

Casa Alberto (C. de las Huertas) is an attractive Spanish restaurant established in 1827, specialising in seafood and meat dishes with home-made vermouth served 'de grifo' (i.e., on tap).

Another theatre with strong ties to royalty and aristocracy is **Teatro**

Calle Mayor, Calderon de la Barca lived in the building on the left.

La Torre del Oro.

Teatro Espanol.

Zarzuela. Founded in the 1650s, it was a favourite venue for works by Lope de Vega and Calderón de la Barca, originally performed at the Palacio de la Zarzuela, near Madrid – home of King Felipe VI and the royal family today. Today's building was constructed in 1856.

La Venencia.

Local eats

La Venencia (C. de Echegaray) is one of the most enchanting of bars in Madrid, selling only five types of Jerez sherry (Manzanilla, Fino, Palo cortado, Amontillado and Oloroso) with cheese, ham and anchovy tapas or raciones. It is another haunt with associations to Hemingway, where east of the battle front line in Madrid, soldiers and journalists would more safely discuss the status of the Siege of Madrid.

Madrid remains Spain's leading centre for theatrical performance and there are tens of theatres to choose from. **Teatro Reina Victoria** opened in 1916 and honours in name Queen Victoria Eugenie, wife of Alfonso XIII (and the granddaughter of Britain's Queen Victoria). **Teatro La Latina** is the most popular place for comedy and review. **Teatro Lara** is an impressive, beautifully designed building, dating from 1879. It hosts a range of performances from musicals and concerts to children's theatre. There are other large theatres, e.g., **Teatro del Canal** and Conde Duque as well as many charming smaller ones (e.g., **Teatro Infanta Isabel)** putting on repertory shows by travelling companies or musical performances. Each maintains Madrid's strong tradition for the performing arts.

THE BOURBONS

Transition to a new dynasty

In 1700, the reckless, corrupt and impoverishing Habsburgs gave way to the more measured, organised and liberal Bourbon dynasty – today, still the constitutional monarchs of Spain despite the tumultuous nineteenth and twentieth centuries.

Upon his death, the childless Charles II bequeathed his inheritance to the French Philip, Duke d'Anjou, grandson of Louis XIV of France, and Charles's sister, Maria Theresa. The inheritance caused great upset in Europe as a French and Spanish union would upset the balance of power. It was a prospect that resulted in the War of Spanish Succession. After a long conflict, it was agreed the Duke d'Anjou could succeed to become Philip V of Spain, but with some major concessions – essentially an agreement not to establish a French–Spanish union, and that Spain should surrender territories to Britain and Austria – the former gaining Gibraltar.

The kingdom of Aragon did not support the succession of Philip V, so it lost out as the Castilian structure of government was promoted. It was a step towards full centralisation completed by later liberal governments. Philip, despite being psychologically troubled and prone to strange behaviours at court, had the presence of mind to borrow aspects of the French model of government. He promoted a cadre of lower nobility to positions of influence to deal directly with him, keeping the entitled upper nobility at arm's length. Fewer foreign ventures, better methods of tax collection and the growing wealth of citizens resulted in a more prosperous state.

In 1724, Philip V abdicated in favour of his son, Louis. However, Louis was a poorly monarch and died young, only reigning for 229 days. His father subsequently returned to the throne and reigned until 1746, followed by his brother Ferdinand VI.

History has judged Ferdinand VI as a wise and just monarch. Whilst not as revered as his younger brother Charles III, Ferdinand created several enlightened institutions in Madrid – most famously the **Real Academia de Bellas Artes de San Fernando**, Madrid's oldest permanent art institution, occupying a converted baroque to neoclassical building on Calle Alcala and holding many works by Goya, Zurbaran, Ribera and Rubens. In later centuries, Francisco Goya would be its director and Salvador Dali a fleeting student before he determined that his style of surrealism was unappreciated by his tutors.

Local eats

El Food Hall de Galería Canalejas (C. de Alcalá) is a modern and stylish gastronomic food court beneath the upmarket fashion mall of the same name. For a special occasion it's hard to beat **Lhardy Restaurante** (C. Carrera de San Jerónimo) – established in 1839, it's one of Madrid's top fine dining experiences, known for Madrileño specialties. An alternative to a main meal are drinks and pastries in the ground floor delicatessen.

In 1755, towards the end of his reign, Ferdinand established the **Real Jardin Botanico**. Today, it is a stunning city-centre oasis and base of scientific research. Completed by his brother Charles III, it was deliberately located next to the Museum of Natural Sciences, the forerunner to the Museo Prado in the same building. Designed by the architects Francesco Sabatini and Juan de Villanueva, it also has some notable structures; principally the Puerta de Murillo, Puerta del Rey and the Villanueva Pavilion. The garden has around 5,500 species of plant (many brought from Spanish colonies

Real Academia de Bellas Artes de San Fernando.

Real Jardin Botanico.

for cultivation). The garden competes with the world-renowned London's Physic and Oxford's Botanic gardens in terms of variety. Originally, it was a working garden providing a supply of medicinal plants to Madrid's general hospital (the Hospital de San Carlos). The hospital closed in 1965, becoming the Museo Reina Sofia in 1992, and the long corridors, large windows and central quadrangle of the museum are all testament to its former life.

Calle del Factor offers tremendous views over the palace, cathedral and beyond to the Casa de Campo and the Sierra de Guadarrama. It is named after the role of a person who manages the financial affairs (i.e., taxes, assets and income) of the king – in this case the 'factor' of Philip II.

Local eats

Restaurante Vegetariano (C. de Santiago) is worth a visit, being one of few vegetarian restaurants in Madrid.

The **Museo de Historia de Madrid** spans the history of the city from the arrival of Philip II (1561) to the present day. Charting the evolution of the Hispanic monarchy, expertly curated paintings, prints and objects explain the story of Madrid. Refurbished in 2014, the museum is housed in the former San Fernando Hospice, designed by Pedro de Ribera – also responsible for the Conde Duque military barracks and both sharing enormous Spanish baroque entrances. A must-see work at the museum is Goya's *Allegory of Madrid* in the War of Independence room.

Local eats

Bodega de la Ardosa (C. de Colon) is an attractive and lively bar with subdued lighting and standing tables. It has a peculiar hidden back bar accessible only by bending under the main bar head down, a unique experience.

Towering over the Manzanares valley, the **Palacio Real de Madrid** is a glittering reminder of the opulence of

Calle del Factor, looking west.

Museo de Historia de Madrid.

Bodega de la Ardosa.

the Bourbon monarchical period – so super-sized is the granite and white-stone architecture, and lavish the interior, that Felippe VI prefers not to live there today. The king, Queen Letizia and Princesses Leonor and Sofia live at the more modest Zarzuela Palace to the west of Madrid. The Palacio is the world's largest palace – stacking over 2,500 rooms on the side of the escarpment that was once home to the Muslim Alcazar.

The Alcazar was built in the 800s as a fortress overlooking the Guadarrama mountains in the north, protecting Toledo in the south. After La Reconquista, successive monarchs tinkered with the building – but at its heart it was no better than a draughty medieval castle – so much so that Philip V's queen (Maria Luisa of Savoy) refused to live there (describing it more colourfully as the 'maison de merde'). She preferred to reside at the nearby Monasterio de las Descalzas Reales. It was little surprise to some that the Alcazar mysteriously burned down on Christmas Eve in 1734, but only once the valuables had been removed. King Philip V, brought up at the Palace of Versailles, engaged Filippo Juvarra (along with his then assistant Juan Battista Sacchetti) to work on a replacement. This is the palace we see today, with some additional work by Francesco Sabatini.

The palace was last inhabited by Alfonso XIII in 1931, preceding the Second Republic, Civil War and Franco's time. Amidst the opulence of the palace's furnishing and fittings are the sword of El Cid (king's champion for the unification and La Reconquista), monarchical armour and priceless musical instruments.

Local eats

La Mi Venta (Pl. de la Marina Espanola) is a long-standing traditional Spanish restaurant and a bit of a local for senators from the nearby Senado. Eating on the terrace provides views of the royal palace, complemented, in the evening, by the setting sun.

Palacio Real de Madrid.

The historic **Jardines del Campo del Moro** cascade down from the Palacio Real toward the River Manzanares. It is a peaceful oasis of lawns, woodlands and monumental fountains today, but once the site of sieges and attacks on the Alcazar during La Reconquista. The land was acquired by Philip II in the late 1500s, and the gardens were developed mainly during the periods of Isabel II and Alfonso XII's regent queen after the king's early death.

Relevo Solemne, Palacio Real de Madrid (first Wednesday of each month).

Jardines del Campo del Moro.

Local eats

Finding a seaside bar experience in Madrid is a tough ask, but the **Café del Rey** (Paseo del Rey) makes a go of it during the summer months with its beach-themed terrace, serving drinks and food that enhance the tropical experience. It has an inside bar for the rest of the year.

Opened in 2023, the magnificent **Galeria de las Colecciones Reales (Royal Collection)** is a grand undertaking by Spain's Patrimonio Nacional. Dug out of the rock underneath the Palacio Real, the gallery is a cultural and historical feast as well as an architectural triumph. The gallery houses the Crown's heritage collection – an idea first mooted during the Second Republic. Treasures span the early reigns of the middle ages up to Juan Carlos I – displayed in three giant exhibition rooms reached by descending a ramped internal promenade. Tapestries, armouries and works of art from the Catholic Monarchs and Habsburgs on floor 1, move to exhibits from the Bourbon period on floor 2 before one arrives in the modern spaces – where immersive media projections display other Patrimonio Nacional sites (e.g., El Escorial).

Local eats

Book the upstairs terrace at **Café del Rio** (Av. de Portugal) and you'll be rewarded with majestic views of the

Galeria de las Colecciones Reales.

royal palace and cathedral perched on the escarpment that is the basis for Madrid's existence. Madrid's rio (i.e., river) is less awe-inspiring, but the authorities have made a tremendous job of making the Manzanares a focal point for family walks and sporting endeavours.

The Mayor King

The reign of Charles III is the most celebrated in Madrid – perhaps of all the Spanish monarchs. Two elder brothers had gone before him and his was a reign that may never have happened, had the elder brothers produced heirs. His initial tenure as King of Naples, a Spanish possession in Italy, had accustomed Charles to the developed infrastructure of that city. On returning to Madrid as the Spanish monarch, Charles was aghast at the inferiority of the national capital. During his 29-year-long reign he pursued a policy of ruthless modernisation and progress – from hospitals to fountains, pavements to ceremonial city gates and 'Aqua Va' (i.e., the warning shouted before waste was despatched from windows) to sewers, rubbish collection and streetlighting. Charles III epitomised reform and enlightenment and lived up to his reputation as the 'Mayor King'. Moreover, he was the first monarch to address the imbalance of land ownership and municipal taxation that favoured the church authorities and nobility – and in the estimates of *La Moncloa*, reducing the number of gentry from 700,000 to 400,000 between 1763 and 1787. Keeping the church out of politics and, with the help of his principal advisor the Count of Floridablanca, the country out of conflicts (in particular, the global Seven Years War), Charles III's legacy was a country moving rapidly to peace and modernity.

Apart from commissioning Juan de Villanueva to rebuild Plaza Mayor in 1790, Charles IV, on succeeding to the throne in 1788, has little to match his father's glorious record of advancement, enlightenment and peace. With his vacant expression (captured well by Goya in family portraits in the Prado), his fate in history was sealed when in 1808, under pressure from Napoleon, he abdicated in favour of his son Ferdinand VII, who then acquiesced and handed the monarchy to Joseph Bonaparte.

In the Malasana district, **Centro Cultural Conde Duque** offers an extensive programme of artistic and cultural performances and events. Managed by Madrid City Council, and covering a giant 60,000 square metres, the site was a military barracks in the 1700s established during the reign of Philip V. In addition to the performing arts, the centre is an important archival centre for Madrid city and Spanish newspapers – plus a lending library

Centro Cultural Conde Duque.

Café Moderno.

and study spaces. The building and its baroque entrance is the work of Pedro de Ribera, also the architect of the Museo de Madrid. The building suffered the ravages of fire and disuse for nearly a century, opening in 2011 as today's centre of culture.

Local eats

La Taberna de Corps (Pl. de los Guardias de Corps) has a privileged location in a quiet square of the arty district of Malasana. The bar is small, but tables extend around the car-free square under the shade of plane trees (the main species of tree in Madrid). For families, also consider the nearby restaurant **Café Moderno** (Pl. de las Comendadoras), located in a large sun-drenched square with play facilities.

Puerta de Sol is the historic centre of Madrid. Today, the large clocktower building is the headquarters of the autonomous Madrid Regional Government, not be confused with the Madrid City Council in Cibeles. The building was formerly the headquarters of the **Real Casa de Correos (Post Office)** from its completion in 1768 to the beginning of the Second Republic in 1931, ensuring that Sol was a focus for the latest news and gossip. During Franco's time, the building was the feared headquarters of the Ministry of the Interior and State Security. As if to claim its centrality in Spain's importance, a stone slab inscribed **Kilometre Zero** stands outside the clocktower building – officially recognised as (nearly) the geographic centre of Spain. Madrid's logo, **El Oso y el Madroño** (the Bear and the Strawberry Tree), and an equestrian statue of Madrid's Mayor King are other prominent landmarks in Sol. Originally, Puerta del Sol was a single gate at the east end of the square, so named for its prominence at dawn – since the morning sun (i.e., sol) would shine through announcing the day. The gate was demolished in the late 1500s to enlarge the square and today's layout dates from the 1860s when Sol became a hub for transport, traders, military mustering and centre of resistance against the Napoleonic invasion – a plaque on the clocktower building marks the centenary of the first engagement of French troops by Spanish patriots on 2 May 1808. Sol is also where the Second Republic was proclaimed in 1931. Today, Sol is a traffic free meeting place notable for the annual New Year's Eve celebrations and the infamous grape-popping as the clock reaches its zenith. To avoid the crush, it is worth enjoying the rehearsal on 30 December.

Local eats

In 1898, Spain's ruling PSOE Party was established in a back room of **Casa Labra** (C. de Tetuan), making a visit for the bar's signature tapas of Bacaloa (i.e., chunks of fried cod) both tasty and historical. Sticking with the fried

Puerta del Sol, statue of Charles III and the former Post Office.

theme, a stand-out (and standing room only) experience can be had at **La Casa del Abuelo** (C. de Victoria), where fried gambas (i.e. prawns) are dished out in high quantities. At weekends, the decibels rise as customers and waiting staff compete to converse and call out orders. It's an experience not to be missed, at this original location of the 'Abuelo' branded bars. For a slightly more sedate time, **Casa Toni** (C. de la Cruz) serves great value Spanish meals at tables – almost always available in the upstairs dining room. Towards the end of the day, **Café Central** (Pl. del Angel) hosts jazz performances

Puerta del Sol.

Casa Labra.

Café Central.

every night by local and international musicians.

Most of the cafes in Sol have gone, except for the popular **La Mallorquina** established in 1894.

The **Museo Nacional de Ciencias Naturales** overlooks the main Paseo de la Castellana city highway. It does a fabulous job of integrating child friendly exhibits on natural history with collections aimed at the more serious enquirer and researcher, especially in the fields of paleobiology and biodiversity. A gallery on the Guadarrama displays the flora and fauna of Madrid's nearby mountain range – explaining lifecycles of many species from wolves to butterflies. Dating from 1771, it is another gift from the reign of Charles III – a special gallery displays his initial objects belonging to the Royal Cabinet.

Local eats

Toppings and Salads (C. del Marqués del Riscal) is an outstanding lunchtime restaurant and counter-service salad bar ideal for families or as a workplace with free Wi-Fi.

Museo Nacional de Ciencias Naturales.

Madrid's most recent of the three major art galleries forming the 'golden triangle' is the **Museo Nacional Thyssen-Bornemisza**. Opened in 1992 and housed in the former eighteenth-century Palacio de Villahermosa, it is an eclectic cross-period collection of works by Baron von Thyssen and family purchased for the nation by the Spanish state. Some critics, whilst admiring the individual works, find the sheer variety on display a little disconcerting, but to others that is the attraction. Over 700 paintings, covering the Old Masters up to 1800, and the Modern Masters of impressionism and the twentieth century are displayed on two floors.

Museo Nacional Thyssen-Bornemisza.

Local eats

Cervantes Cerveceria (Pl. Jesús) offers table, bar or street terrace service with a menu of fine Spanish meals. On Sundays, it's enlightening to watch customers spill out of the church opposite (Basílica de Jesús de Medinaceli) and onto the terrace of the Cervecería.

Today, four monumental city gates from the modern (i.e., Bourbon) period remain standing. These are: **Puerta de Hierro**, **Puerta de Alcala**, **Puerta de Toledo**, **Puerta de San Vicente**. Puerta de Alcala is the largest and most celebrated gate and claims to be Europe's first triumphal arch. Approaching from outside the city, the five-arched gate welcomes visitors with sculptures of cherubs, whilst upon departure we are greeted by soldiers and military icons – reminding the visitor of the city's prowess and authority. Commissioned, like San Vicente, by Charles III (Hierro and Toledo were both commissioned by Ferdinand VI), it's a neo-classical design by the master of royal works, Francesco Sabatini, dating from 1780. Best seen illuminated at dusk.

Local eats

For a break from shopping in the Salamanca district and an opportunity for relaxing, **Verso y Veta** (C. de Lagasca) is an upmarket cafe and jamon retailer, with a bright aspect onto the streets.

Opposite Ventura Rodriguez metro station is a stately building designed by the man of the same name who designed the **Palacio de Liria**, completed in 1785. Today's building is substantially renovated following a devastating fire in 1936. The palace is the home of the nineteenth Duke of Alba, one of Europe's most titled aristocratic families and owners of an outstanding art collection with works by the Spanish old masters (e.g., Velázquez, Murillo, Zurbaran, El Greco and Ribera) plus by Rubens, Titian and Goya. Famously, on display in the library is a first edition of *Don Quixote* and the world's largest collection of handwritten letters, charts and notes from Christopher Columbus. The original Madrid residence of the House of Alba, before moving to Palacio de Liria, was the Palacio de Buenavista, now the Army Headquarters opposite Plaza Cibeles.

Housed in the mammoth former Hospital San Carlos (established during the reign of Philip II but extended in 1787 by Charles III with the court-favourite architect Francesco Sabatini), the **Museo Nacional Centro de Arte Reina Sofia** is a triumphal collection of art, concentrating on works between 1900–1982. Opened in 1990, it is the centre for works by Spain's principal

Puerta de Alcala.

Palacio de Liria.

modern masters (e.g., Pablo Picasso, Salvador Dali and Juan Miro) as well as many international modern artists. The 2005 Nouvel extension showcases art from the 1960s–80s. Arguably, the museum's most famous work is *Guernica* by Picasso, commissioned by the Republican Government for the Paris Exhibition of 1937. The large canvas portrays the bombing of the Spanish northern town by Nationalist forces during the Spanish Civil War (although the imagery is from similar atrocities in Madrid and Malaga). The Reina's two satellite galleries (the Velazquez Palace and the Crystal Palace) are in the Retiro.

Local eats

NuBel (Reina Sofia) is a stylish venue for a coffee or meal with, at the weekends, a DJ playing cool vibes consistent with the gallery's contemporary art collections. **Mercado de Anton Martin** (C. de Santa Isabel) hosts many shops and bars frequented by cool hipster customers on this desirable street, managing to maintain a free-spirited vibe. Leading a host of bars on C. de Santa Isabel,

Nacional Centro de Arte Reina Sofia.

NuBel.

Bar Benteveo harks back to the seventies with its red Formica bar and traditional furnishings.

Situated on the **Paseo del Prado** between the Cibeles and Neptune fountains (both designed by Ventura Rodriguez in the late 1780s to supply local needs), the **Museo Nacional del Prado** is one of the world's great art galleries – and the pre-eminent collection of the early Spanish masters. The earlier works are largely thanks to the collecting tradition established by Philip II and adopted by subsequent monarchs. It's the undisputed go-to gallery for works by Diego Velazquez and Francisco Goya, both of whom are buried in the capital. Goya's tomb can be visited, but Velazquez is lying somewhere in the city, having a memorial in Plaza Ramales marking the likely location. Originally conceived by Philip II, the Paseo is the world's most famous tree-lined boulevard. Renowned for the elaborate social rites displayed by the wealthy engaging in an evening paseo, the boulevard was built over a meadow, taking its name, Prado, in Spanish.

Local eats

Taberna La Daniela (Pl. Jesus) is one of four restaurants by the same name, providing Madrid gastronomy in a traditional tavern setting with cool blue and yellow tilework.

Museo Nacional del Prado.

The Prado was originally conceived by Charles III as a museum of natural sciences. The neo-classical building by Juan de Villanueva dates from 1785. Damaged by Napoleon's troops, who used the building as a munitions store, it was restored by Ferdinand VII as a museum to house the royal art collection. Opening as a museum of art to the public in 1819, the Prado houses thousands of paintings, drawings, prints and sculptures – boasting more than 100 works by Goya and 50 by Velazquez. Outside, statues of the two great artists claim their manor.

With an almost overwhelming choice, no visit to the Prado would be complete without seeing the fascinating, technical and amusing painting *Les Meninas* by Velazquez (1656) – argued as the world's finest early modern work of art, placing the viewer in the heart of the painting.

Goya's royal portraits, indicating a certain disdain for Charles IV and his almost pornographic *Naked Maja*, lost him his role as court painter. His Dark Paintings were produced towards the end of his life. Painted when he was deaf, and not intended for public display, these were lifted off the walls of his residence in the west of Madrid, applied to canvas and displayed in the museum.

Other must-sees are *The Garden of Earthly Delights* (1503–15) by Hiëronymus Bosch, *Self Portrait* (1498) by Albrecht Durer, *The Three Graces* (1630–35) by Rubens and works by Raphael, Titian and Caravaggio. Nearby, the Cason del Buen Retiro (former ballroom of Philip IV's palace) houses an impressive collection of nineteenth century art.

Local eats

It can be intimidating to cross the threshold of **La Dolores Bar** (Pl. Jesus) when it's in full swing but persevere for a warm welcome and a range of delicious bar tapas. Forget about trying to find a seat and crush up the long bar, order a cana (i.e., a small beer on tap,

La Dolores Bar.

Palacio de Linares.

pronounced 'can-ya') or vermut and soak up the atmosphere.

The Prado has no works of the cubist, abstract or surrealist periods – but the works of Picasso, Miro and Dali are in abundance at the Museo Nacional Centro de Arte Reina Sofía. However, a single painting bridging the early period and the twentieth century is Joaquín Sorolla's most famous work, *Boys on the Beach* (1909).

Opposite Cibeles Place, the **Palacio de Linares** (1877) was designed for the noble Linares family and sumptuously decorated in Louis XV and Rococo designs – it is one of the best conserved nineteenth-century mansions in Europe showing off eclectic styles and opulent plasterwork – possibly a little over-the-top for some tastes. Today, it is the Casa de America, hosting artistic and cultural events relating to the Americas.

Despotic rule

Charles IV had thought it a good idea to invite Napoleon into Spain, to jointly attack Portugal and its ally, England. What he did not count on was that this would trigger the start of six years of French occupation, ceding the monarchy to Napoleon's brother, Joseph. It would herald the start of the War of Independence.

Once the French were defeated in 1814, Ferdinand VII reclaimed the throne and returned to the died-in-the-wool absolutist tyrant he was, reinstating the inquisition and closing the university in Madrid because of its liberal views. In 1812, whilst under occupation by the French, representatives in Cadiz had declared a national parliament, liberal constitution and passed progressive laws that promoted equality and democracy of all citizens. Ferdinand closed this parliament, repealed the new laws and rounded up the leaders.

Supported by France and Britain, Ferdinand survived a popular uprising and military coup that introduced a more liberal constitution between 1820–1823, having its leader Colonel Rafael del Riego executed. On a more positive note, he repealed Salic Law to permit female succession and unintentionally boosted the stock of works at the Prado – if only to make way for the latest French wallpaper in the royal palace.

The **Ateneo de Madrid** is Madrid's longest standing cultural institution.

Library, Ateneo de Madrid.

Opened in 1835 after the death of Ferdinand VII, it represented a fresh move towards more tolerant liberal attitudes. Consistent to its founding principles, with some interruptions during dictatorships (i.e., Miguel Primo de Rivera and Francisco Franco), it offers an almost-daily programme of new lectures, recitals and exhibitions. The members-only library (which can be glimpsed on the second floor) looks straight out of a film set.

Local eats

If you haven't booked for an event, **La Cantina at Ateneo de Madrid** is open to all, offering bar classics and fine dining on the 'Segunda Planta'.

Towering over Plaza de Oriente, the **Teatro Real (Royal Theatre)** is one of Europe's leading opera houses and performance venues. Conceived during the reign of Ferdinand VII and built from 1818, it was opened by his daughter Isabella II in 1850. The theatre was part of an overall remodelling of the plaza, favoured by the French during the years of occupation.

Local eats

Café del Oriente (Pl. de Oriente), an upmarket café with a prime location on the plaza, is perfect for views of the Bourbon Royal Palace and (appropriately) French cuisine and watching other, albeit mostly international travellers, enjoying the scenes.

Ateneo de Madrid.

Teatro Real.

Café del Oriente.

Taste of reform

Ferdinand VII died in 1833 and the throne passed to his three-year-old infant daughter Isabella II. At succession her mother (Maria Christina de Borbon) was regent until 1843 when Isabella reached majority age.

From the start, her rule was disputed by Ferdinand's brother Don Carlos – believing he was the rightful heir. It would be the start of the Carlist Wars, Spain's first Civil War. Splitting the nation equally they ran the entirety of her reign (to 1868), that of her successor Amadeo (to 1873), the brief first republic (to 1874) and the early years of Alfonso XII's subsequent reign up to 1876.

Isabella II, taking note of the success of the French Revolution, started out an enlightened and moderate monarch desiring a more equal society, like Britain. The liberal constitution of 1837 had already passed laws on land redistribution, driving free market concepts, and during her personal reign Isabella invested in popular improvements like railways and water supply – Madrid's water company still goes by her name.

Later in her reign, ultimately failing to keep pace with the demands of a more expectant electorate, whose hopes had been whetted by the initial reforms, liberalism took a back seat. Isabella became more interfering and authoritarian, relied on a cadre of

Palacio de la Cortes.

miliary officers and passed legislation that smacked of gerrymandering, aimed at keeping the ruling party in power. Questionable morals in her private life provided more ammunition for her detractors. In the end, Isabella II was overthrown by a military coup in 1868 and went into exile in France.

Spain's Parliament (The Cortes Generales) comprises a lower house of the Congreso de los Diputados (i.e., Congress of Deputies, the MPs) and an upper house of the Senado (i.e., Senate). The lower house is based in the **Palacio de la Cortes** near the Jerónimos district and the **Senate** is based in **Palacio del Senado**, near Plaza Espana. The Senate can review, reflect on and request second readings of bills, but the final decisions rest with the Congress. The Senate also has a role to bridge the interests of Spain's Self-Governing-Communities with central Government. Both houses were established by Royal Statute in 1834 and held powers depending on the constitution in place at the time. Seats were initially awarded based on birth-right or royal appointment, until universal suffrage was introduced with the Second Republic in 1931, although without a Senate. After Franco's time, the Political Reform Act of 1977 transitioned the Cortes to the model today.

The neoclassical Palacio de la Cortes, completed in 1850, is guarded by two external bronze lions known as Daoiz y Velarde after two of the resistance heroes of the War of Independence. The Senate was housed in a former Augustinian convent from the 1700s – but now extensively renovated and extended, most recently with the addition of a new building in 1987 (i.e., the rounded façade at its rear). A failed military coup that took place in 1981 in the Congress of Deputies building by some low-level colonels disaffected with democracy and seeking a return to Francoism is an image still fresh in the minds of parliamentarians. Juan Carlos I lost no time in distancing himself from the coup live on television and the constitution survived. The bullet holes in the ceiling, fired as warning shots, were deliberately retained for 40 years after the shootings – but are now mostly covered over to prevent leaks.

Palacio del Marques de Salamanca is the former residence of the Marquis of Salamanca – the driving force and primary investor in the Salamanca district. Completed in 1855, today it is the headquarters of the BBVA Foundation, funding research in the fields of environment, science, technology and society and a centre

Palacio del Senado.

Café Gijon.

for year-round cultural events and exhibitions. Standing prominently on Paseo de Recoletos, the building also reminds us of the wealth and standing of Spain's aristocracy in the nineteenth century.

Local eats

An esteemed café, established in 1888, **Café Gijon** (Paseo de Recoletos) reached its zenith as Madrid's foremost literary café for intellectuals and creatives collectively known as the generation of '36 – a reference to the year the Spanish Civil War commenced. Later it became a haunt of foreign writers and stars. Food is excellent, service exudes no nonsense old-world charm, whilst the brightly lit original interior distinguishes it from a host of blander, modern restaurants.

Road to the First Republic

General Prim led the coup against Isabella II and initiated popular measures such as universal male suffrage and religious freedom – all groundbreaking progress. He passed the crown to Amadeo of Savoy (son of

Victor Emanuelle of Italy), a man who, failing to grasp the nettle of Spanish government, sought the middle ground and only upset both the left and the right.

In 1873, Amadeo abdicated and cooly exiled himself. Leaving a vacuum, the Cortes proclaimed the First Republic. Progressive, but trying to achieve too much too young – a theme that would also fracture the Second Republic in 1931 – the republic only lasted twenty-two months.

Unhappy with the pace of change and mistrusting those in power, General Pavia led a further military coup in 1874, perhaps energised by the army having mortally defeated the Carlists at San Pedro Abanto (near Segovia) the same year, resulting in their elimination two years later. Since nobody wished the return of Isabella II, Pavia installed Isabella's son Alfonso XII as the new monarch. This event is known as the Bourbon Restoration. Tumultuous as it had been between 1868 and 1874, the period did see Spain progress toward economic liberalisation and equality and is referred to today as the 'Sexenio Democrático'.

Restoration and progress

Liberals, and the population at large, were content with Alfonso XII as the constitutional monarch, being seen as a middle ground between more radical alternatives – more inclusive than absolutism and less worrying than a republic. It was a system that would last until 1931. The constitution of 1876 also mandated a rotation of power between the conservative and liberal parties. Despite rigging, it was a form of political stability that would continue until 1902 (when Alfonso XIII reached majority age).

It was a febrile period of political ideas and leaders with many new parties being formed and regional independence rising as a hot issue. The Partido Socialista Obrero Espanol (PSOE), the Spanish Socialist Workers Party, was founded in 1879 (out of early meetings in Café Labra) and around a decade later the UGT (Unión General de Trabajadores), the General Workers Union, was founded – finding strong support from Madrid's printers, miners in Asturias and industrial workers in the Basque Country. These were joined by the separatist parties for Basque (1895) and Catalonia (1901) – the Communist party was a relative latecomer, founded in 1921.

Alfonso XII died young in 1885, at the age of 28. His infant son was given the crown, whilst his mother, Maria Christina of Austria, acted as regent until the boy reached majority age in 1902. He is remembered favourably by history and his giant equestrian statue towers over the lake in the Retiro.

Still an unequal country, the main challenges were dealing with the separatists, the demands of the political parties and the new trade union movements of the working class – themes that would propel Spain into the modern era with long-lasting consequences.

Equal universal male suffrage had returned in 1890. Prior to that, between 1870–1890, male suffrage had been based on a 'censitary' system, meaning the higher your rank the more votes you had. Women had to wait until 1931 for the vote (shocking, but in Britain it was only three years earlier). New found power at the ballot box raised the expectations of the male working classes, demands the state found difficult to fund.

Throughout the nineteenth century, Spain's empire had withered away, and then disappeared altogether in 1898 with the loss of the Philippines and Cuba, spawning a national seizure among the so-called 'Generation of '98'. The absence of funds from an empire, limited natural resources and a relatively poor industrial base put a cap on how progressive the state could be. The wealth and loucheness of the aristocracy and endemic corruption among the ruling classes worsened matters. The proletariat was restless for change and watched with interest the success of the Russian Revolution in 1917.

Always a militaristic leader, Alfonso XIII became increasingly autocratic later in his reign. Breaching his constitutional mandate, violently putting down strikes and resorting to executions to quell social unrest, he started to lose his legitimacy. He narrowly survived an assassination attempt in 1906 on him and his new queen Victoria Eugenie of Battenberg, a granddaughter of Britain's Queen Victoria (their survival is commemorated by a statue in Calle Mayor). Despite him later keeping Spain out of World War I (resulting in an unexpected economic boom for Spain), many citizens turned against him.

The final tipping point was the massacre of besieged Spanish troops in the 1921 Riff War in Morocco – during which an estimated 14,000 trapped Spanish troops were slaughtered by Berber tribesmen. Alfonso XIII had thought the reassertion of the Spanish Protectorate in north Morocco would bring pride back to the country following the loss of its other colonies, but instead it was a defeat that brought shame on the army, criticism of the Government and solicited widespread disgust at the loss of young lives.

The white-stone **Palacio de Cibeles** (1919) is a cathedral-like edifice and the first commission of Spain's most famous modern-age architect: Antonio Palacios. Originally the central post office, it is now home to Madrid City Council and a public exhibition space **(Centro Centro)** with a 360-degree roof-top terrace.

Local eats

Upstairs, the sixth floor **Azotea Cibeles** is a modern roof top space, with fabulous views over Madrid, serving coffees, cocktails and cakes.

An unmissable sight is the building designed in 1919 as the Madrid headquarters of the **BBVA Bank**. Now the headquarters of the **Ministerio de Agricultura**, the building cuts a dash with two enormous roof-top chariots pulled by four horses (i.e., a quadriga). Once gold, the bronzes were painted black during the Civil War to prevent them being beacons for aerial bombardment, and have remained so in memory of those dark days.

Instituto Cervantes has been promoting the study and teaching of the Spanish language and Hispanic culture worldwide since it was founded in 1991. The Madrid headquarters is a former bank, also designed by Antonio Palacios and completed in 1918. It hosts regular free exhibitions, which also provides the opportunity to see the lavish marble former banking hall. Opposite the institute, the headquarters of **El Edificio del Banco de**

Palacio de Cibeles.

Palacio de Cibeles.

Ministerio de Agricultura.

Espana, designed by Eduardo de Adaro and completed in 1891, is a reassuring hunk of a building holding Spain's reserves of gold.

Local eats

For value for money in the centre of Madrid, it's hard to beat **El Tigre Sidreria** (C. de Hortaleza), serving giant portions of complimentary tapas – so much so you're in danger of spoiling your appetite if dining later. The atmosphere is energetic, as patrons catch up whilst gorging on the moreish fried food.

The **Museo Lazaro Galdiano** is the former residence of the publisher and art collector of the same name and one of Madrid's finest smaller galleries. The stately building and grounds were constructed in 1903 and today exhibit Galdiano's important collection of paintings and manuscripts. The collector died in 1947 and donated his collection to the state, which opened it to the public in 1951. The art includes works by the Spanish masters Velazquez, El Greco, Ribera and Goya plus works by Bosch Rembrandt, Gainsborough and Turner.

Below left: ***Instituto Cervantes, from Circulo de Bellas Artes.***

Below right: ***El Edificio del Banco de Espana.***

Local eats

Taberna O'Caldino (C. de Lagasca) is one of Madrid's finest restaurants, known especially for its Galician cuisine and seafood served in an atmospheric old-world decor. For a light bite, enjoy a glass of wine at the bar, accompanied by any variety of shell fish from the counters.

The magnificent **Plaza de Espana** is a large public space hosting open-air events throughout the year and a meeting place for families near the Royal Palace, equipped with children's play facilities. Opened in 1911, the large central statue of Spain's renowned writer Miguel Cervantes was added four years later, accompanied by statues of his most famous creations of Don Quixote and Sancho Panza dating from 1930.

Local eats

Mercado Los Mostenses (P. de los Mostenses) is an experience not to be missed. Only yards from the

Museo Lazaro Galdiano.

Taberna O'Caldino.

Plaza de Espana.

swish environs of the Gran Via, it's a workers' food market. One eye-popping meat counter offers all types of meat offal.

The **Museo Cerralbo** is presented in the state it was left in 1922 by the Marquis of Cerralbo. A grand staircase, mirrored ballroom, works by the Spanish greats (e.g., El Greco, Cano and Zurbaran) plus a collection of weapons make the house a vivid example of how nobility used to live in Madrid.

Local eats

Nearby, **Ocho y Medio Cinema Books Bar** (C. de Martín de los Heros) is an Aladdin's cave of film and tv books, scripts and ephemera, with a bar serving snacks and drinks. After a couple of wines, the film posters signed

Museo Cerralbo.

El Estadio Santiago Bernabeu.

by Pedro Almodovar, Javier Bardem or Penelope Cruz begin to look great value.

Judged by the silverware on display in the museum and being a 12 times European Cup winner, Real Madrid was declared the best club in the history of football in 1988. The club was founded in 1902, and the 80,000-seater, multi-purpose **El Estadio Santiago Bernabeu** stadium (built in 1947) was named after its illustrious president in 1955.

Estacion de Atocha is Spain's largest railway station. Built in 1851, its vast wrought iron canopy was the work of designers Alberto de Palacio and Elissague and Gustave Eiffel (who later designed the Eiffel Tower). The canopy now houses an indoor tropical garden, facing a large cylindrical monument in memory of the deaths of 193 people following a terrorist attack on 11 March 2004.

Mirroring Atocha in the north, is Madrid's station for northern destinations, **Estacion de Principe Pio.** This is a scaled down version of its former self – the freed-up space

Estacion de Atocha.

now hosting a complex of retail and performance venues. Completed in 1917, its ironwork interior is a reminder of the days of steam.

Local eats

Amidst the cavernous space, numerous modern eateries congregate to form a giant food-hall.

One of Madrid's most delightful house museums, **Museo Sorolla**, charts the life of Joaquin Sorolla y Bastida through his art and in his home, where he worked and lived from 1911 to 1923. Famed for being the Spanish 'painter of light', his impressionistic style and ability to capture the tones of the Mediterranean coastline around Valencia, makes him one of Spain's most loved early twentieth-century artists. See works such as *Walk by the sea* (1909) – the painter's most representative style depicting his wife and daughter walking along the beach in Valencia. Sorolla commissioned the building of the house in 1909 and personally designed the garden, a serene spot in the city centre.

Museo Sorolla.

Local eats

El Horno (C. de Zurbano) is another excellent café serving all types of pastries, and with free Wi-Fi is very suitable as a work-café.

If you have a head for heights, the **Sala Canal de Isabel II** is a unique space hosting progressive and avant-garde audio-visual and photographic exhibitions inside a former water tower. The tower once provided the pressure for abundant water in the north of Madrid and is named after the former monarch who funded the building of a canal to supply water to the city from the Guadarrama mountains in the 1850s. The tower, built in 1911, is an exhilarating example of industrial architecture.

Gran Via was conceived as an east-west artery to ease congestion in the city. At its southern end the style resembles the picturesque French fin-de-siecle (e.g., **Edificio**

Sala Canal de Isabel II.

Grassy, Gran Via, 1), in the middle section American Art Nouveau and Art Deco styles are introduced, whilst the northern end gives way to post-war styles reminiscent of New York City's Broadway, in both style and purpose. Carving its way through central Madrid, Gran Via took 30 years to build. Conceived in 1890 and shortening or destroying more than 50 streets, work eventually began in 1910 (at the southern end), then 1917 (in the middle section) and completed with the northern end in 1929. At its centre the Edificio Telefonica towers over the city – an astonishing architectural achievement that made it Europe's tallest skyscraper when it was erected in 1929. Erected at the start of the Gran Via and junction with C. de Alcala, **Edificio Metropolis** is one of Madrid's most recognisable and iconic sights, an image of the Belle Epoque deployed thousands of times in postcards. Designed by Jules y Raymond Ferrier, and inaugurated in 1911 as an insurance company headquarters, its black slate roof is topped by a winged figure of Victory. The best (free) view of Gran Via can be had from the 9th floor café of **El Corte Ingles** (C. de Preciados) – Spain's undisputed leader of department stores founded as a small tailoring business in 1890, calling itself 'The English Cut'. Emphasizing the political turbulence of the Civil War and its aftermath, the street was only returned to its original name in the 1980s, having been renamed by the Republican Government in 1931 and then the Franco regime in the 1940s.

Local eats

Many to choose, but at the southern end, **Museo Chicote** (Gran Via) is Madrid's first and most famous cocktail bar, built in 1931. It was immortalised by artists and film stars from the 1950s; you may enjoy sitting in the favoured seats and barstools of Ava Gardner, Sophia Loren, Frank Sinatra and others. In the middle section: **Rodilla** (Pl. del Calloa) is the original shop of the widespread sandwich chain and in the northern section **Los Entendidos** (Gran Via) provides a seated and pavement service for two of the city's most popular quick bites – a Bocadillo de Calamares and Churros y Chocolate.

In common with much of Europe, the period also experienced an ignition of retail as a functional and leisure activity. Established in 1882, **Guitarras Ramirez** is Madrid's oldest and most regarded Spanish guitar retailer. The shop, on a quiet street near the Barrio de Letras, is a cornucopia of guitar types and ephemera – an homage for enthusiasts. Equally for the dedicated, the 150-year-old **Casa de Diego** is the most authentic and memorable place to purchase their self-produced fans – with sidelines in umbrellas and walking sticks.

Edificio Metropolis from Circulo de Bellas Artes.

Museo Chicote.

Above left: ***Edificio Grassy.***

Above right: ***Café El Corte Ingles, Preciados.***

Local eats

Based on the site of a former church to San Miguel, reduced to a public square with an open-air market when the church burned down, the **Mercado de San Miguel** (Pl de San Miguel) was built in 1916 as an indoor market, replacing the former space and providing an alternative to the market in Puerta del Sol. Its airy iron architecture was an innovation at the time and it continues to lead the field as a gastro-market for well-healed Madrileños and tourists seeking gourmet treats.

THE MODERN ERA

The mild despot

Sensing the time was right and with the acquiescence of Alfonso XIII, General Miguel Primo de Rivera staged a military coup in 1921 and installed a military government. Promising to rule as dictator for 90 days only, he remained in power for nine years.

Primo de Rivera attempted to fix several political and structural problems. He ended the Moroccan War and instructed works on investments ranging from public infrastructure to universities. His style has been termed 'mild despotism', faithful to the monarch and trying to navigate Spain through difficult political times.

By 1930, despite progress on infrastructure, the lack of support from businesses and workers compounded the failing Spanish economy. Governmental corruption and a dictator state turned many against the regime. More gallingly for Primo personally, there were anti-government demonstrations by intellectuals and students at Madrid University – a product of his regime. Fainthearted support from other generals and intellectuals (like Jose Ortega y Gasset, Georgio Marañón and Pérez de Ayala), all calling for a republic, signalled the end. Primo resigned in January 1930, went into exile in France and died shortly thereafter in Paris.

Primo's resignation heralded elections, for which Alfonso XIII (who never abdicated during the dictatorship) expected to be returned in the role of absolute monarch. Alfonso lost and the Second Republic was overwhelmingly proclaimed by the people in 1931.

Primo's son, Jose Antonio Primo de Rivera, would never forgive the generals that ruined his father's regime. He went on to found and lead the right-wing Falange party that played a key role in the run up to, prosecution and aftermath of the Civil War.

The Apple Store in Puerta del Sol was formerly the **Hotel Paris** (1864-2006), a favourite meeting place for Primo and his supporters. Its large ground floor hosted the reception and lounge, whilst the first floor was home to a 500-seat restaurant, Madrid's largest. The famous **Tio Pepe** neon sign was originally located above the building.

Tio Pepe, Puerta de Sol.

Local eats

Antonio Palacios was also responsible for designing the **Círculo de Bellas Artes** (1926). Once an art-school attended by Pablo Picasso, it now hosts cultural events and has a thriving roof terrace with a bar, restaurant and great views.

The **Museo del Romanticismo** is an homage to the romantic aesthetic of the mid-to-late nineteenth century,

Roof terrace, Círculo de Bellas Artes.

showcasing beautifully set rooms decorated in the period, concentrating on Isabelline and imperial furnishings. Established in 1924 the museum is housed in a typical Madrileño building constructed a century earlier for the Marquis of Matallana.

Local eats

Petisqueria II (C. de Mejía Lequerica) is one of Madrid's best tapas bars, serving large complimentary portions of whatever tapas emanates from chef's kitchen every ten minutes or so. On weekend evenings the whole bar drops into another gear as the diverse clientele congregates in every available cornice. If you would prefer a less bustling venue, nearby **Cerveceria Santa Barbara** (Pl. de Santa Barbara) offers a more sedate, but equally castizo, experience with table service.

The opening of an important new **Plaza de Toros Las Ventas** (i.e., bullring) was a populist move by Miguel Primo de Rivera. Commissioned in 1929, its

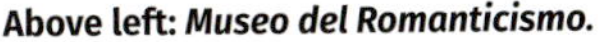

Above left: ***Museo del Romanticismo.***

Above right: ***Cerveceria Santa Barbara.***

Plaza de Toros Las Ventas.

Plaza de Toros Las Ventas.

neo-Mudejar architectural style evokes the bullrings found in southern Spain, and Madrid's is the largest in the country. Scene of much excitement and death (usually around eight bulls per event), the museum explains the history of this complex sport.

The Second Republic

During the seventeenth and eighteenth centuries, the abundance of silver flowing in from Latin America stifled indigenous industry – as Jeremy Black notes, much like how oil has stifled diversified economies in the oil-rich countries of the Middle East. The silver created inequality and class division in Spain on a scale greater than elsewhere in Europe. The people of France dealt with the class system with the French Revolution (1789), whilst Britain's Civil Wars (1642–51), Glorious Revolution (1660) and Industrial Revolution (c. 1760–1830) redistributed wealth, levelled the playing field and created an aspiring class, whilst her empire fuelled the economy and funded infrastructure, education and social improvement, measures that foiled any enthusiasm for strife among the proletariat. Spain had no such cultural or economic transformation and in the light of the successful Russian Revolution in 1917 it was a powder keg of discontent.

The resignation of the opulent Alfonso XIII and the subsequent dictatorship of Miguel Primo de Rivera was an attempt to narrow the class divide. But after ten years of failed economic policies, governmental corruption and a military coup favouring a republic, Primo de Rivera had resigned.

Spain was polarised politically: the left seeking fundamental changes in equality and the economic system whilst the right tried to preserve the old order. On the left stood the socialists, communists and anarchists, covering a spectrum of demands ranging from labour reform to the abolition of private property. The right watched the backs of the wealthy, landowners, aristocracy, monarchists and the church, while the army stood for Spain and a forlorn return to worldwide influence, with most officers holding conservative views.

On the left, the socialists rallied around the PSOE, the communists to the POUM (Partido Obrero de Unificación Marxista – the Workers Party of Marxist Unification) and the anarchists with the CNT (Confederación Nacional del Trabajo). Taking an active part in politics (and later conflict) was the largest left-wing union, UGT led by Francisco Cabellero, dubbed Spain's Lenin.

On the right, the two main proponents were CEDA (Confederación Española de Derechas Autónomas) – the Spanish Confederation of Autonomous Rights led by José María

Gil-Robles and the Falangists led by Jose Antonio Primo de Rivera (son of the dictator Miguel). The Falangists were young radicals seeking a totalitarian government, identified by their blue shirts and an emblem of red arrows (still seen around Madrid as bill stickers today), saluting to the sound of the anthem *Face the Sun*. Dramatic posters extolling these political parties hang in the Museo Nacional Centro de Arte Reina Sofía.

In April 1931, the electorate, despising Alfonso XIII for foisting a military dictatorship on the country, returned a socialist republican government, achieved through a coalition of the left-wing parties. Strident in its approach, the Government set about to implement a wide-ranging set of reforms aimed at creating a fairer and more secular modern state. Forced land purchase and redistribution to the poor, compulsory free education, a reduced army, civil marriage and legal divorce, and the freeing of 30,000 prisoners incarcerated during Primo's regime pleased intellectuals, workers, radicals and the poor – but scared elites, landowners, the church and, critically, many officers in the army.

Holding together the Popular Front coalition of CNT anarchists, far-left POUM (Trotskyite) and the PSUC (Partido Socialista Unificado de Cataluña) seeking communist-style centralisation, whilst promoting a liberal democracy, was a near-impossible task for Prime Minister Niceto Alcalá Zamora (also President of the Second Republic between 1931 and 1936) followed by Prime Minister Manuel Azana. Stable government was not assisted by the CNT and POUM, who prioritised revolution over all else. Arguably pouring oil on troubled waters, the left-wing Government created a secular public education system that precluded all monks and nuns from teaching, banned the crucifix in schools and forbade public processions of Catholicism – all radical and divisive policies, heightened by a dramatic reduction in spending on the army. Further adding to emotions, and aiming to hang onto power, the Government pushed through statutes of autonomy for Catalonia and the Basque Country. Despite some progressive social and egalitarian policies, internal political division and high levels of corruption were the death knell for the Republican Government.

In December 1933, the people voted the left-wing Government out in favour of the right-wing CEDA confederation under Prime Minister Alejandro Lerroux García. The new Government slowed the pace of change and repealed several laws. The rowing-back on progressive policies (such as agrarian reform), bitterly displeased the working class, leading to a general strike by socialist, communist and anarchist workers. The Miners' Revolutionary Strike in 1934, (centred in Asturias) was particularly effective and in consequence was brutally put down by the military under Francisco Franco, resulting in 2,000 civilian deaths. The right-wing Government could only achieve majority through coalitions with the centre and moderate left. Found to be equally corrupt, it lost to the left-wing in subsequent elections.

In February 1936, returning to power, the left-wing Popular Front moved ahead with its prior reforms. A state education system was set up, 10,000 schools opened and home rule granted in Catalonia and the Basque Country. Once again, party-political fragmentation meant that majority could only be achieved through deal making – diluting reforms and creating a torpor on the ground that failed to please anyone on either the left or the right. The socialists sought progressive change, the communists waited for a peoples' revolution whilst the anarchists sought abolition of the state altogether. Divided they stood and divided they would fall – to the pleasure of CEDA and the Falange, eulogising over a proud New Spain that embraced the valour of the Christian Monarchs.

Prime Minister Manuel Azana was despised by the political right and left; his desire for negotiation being seen as promoting not only a corrupt liberal system but a godless republic. Matters escalated in 1936 with the burning of churches, murders of clerics and pitched street battles between opposing factions in the provincial capitals. The church became a target, partly for its wealth, but mainly for the intransigence of its clerics to the plight of the poor – some clerics preaching from the pulpit that if there was inequality it must be the will of God. The Government was largely viewed as standing by, acquiescent, as churches burned.

The long period of Republican Government was considered as corrupt and damaging, resulting in not only the breakdown of social order but fragmentation of the country and marginalisation of the Catholic Church. Harking back again to the values of early Christian Spain, the military staged a *coup d'etat*. It failed but led the country into a brutal three-year-long Spanish Civil War.

The **Viaducto de Segovia** is an impressive 35-metre-high concrete arched bridge, connects the Royal Palace with the **Jardín de las Vistillas** (Pl. de Gabriel Miro) and routes south out of the city. The current viaduct dates from 1931, replacing a former bridge from 1874. From its centre-point, it offers fine views of the royal palace, cathedral, the Casa de Campo and west to the Guadarrama mountains. The viaduct conveys the steepness of the escarpment upon which the palace is built and the age-old engineering problem of creating a route south from the palace.

Jardín de las Vistillas.

Local eats

Making a break from purely Madrid cuisine, **La Taberna Sanlúcar** (C. de San Isidro Labrador) is a typical southern-Spain tavern transporting diners to the port of Cadiz, with Jerez sherry and a menu of Andalusian dishes.

Regarded by many as Madrid's finest residential plaza, **Plaza de Olavide** was home to a large concrete mercado created during the Second Republic, until it was demolished in the early 1970s. Today, it is a beautiful, landscaped octagonal space with a central playground surrounded by numerous bars and restaurants – and an ideal place to sample the city-centre family living experience of Madrileños.

Plaza de Olavide.

Local eats

The plaza is bustling with bars and restaurants, so you are spoilt for choice. On weekend evenings things can get busy, so if you find yourself struggling to get seated, perch outside **Kybey II** (Calle de Palafox) with the throng of locals.

The long Franco period

Upon defeating the forces of the Republican Government, Franco and his regime spent the long aftermath of the Civil War hunting down its enemies, whether leaders of opposition parties, trade unions, town council officials or journalists – settling scores and eliminating future dissention. It's believed that around 50,000 people met their fate in front of Fascist Government firing squads during this period.

Exhausted and broke, the country declared neutrality in World War II but remained aligned with Hitler and Mussolini – changing time zones to match those of Germany and Italy, an anomaly that remains to this day, soliciting a high price for Madrid's welcome light winter evenings.

From a low base, industry and agriculture regressed and war-time rationing ravaged the country. Perversely, the defeat of Germany and Italy gave an unexpected economic boost, allowing Spain to write off Civil War debts owed to them. This was fortuitous, since being an isolated and autocratic country, Spain was cut off from post-war funds of the US Marshall Plan.

The centrality of the Church was reinstated, unions were banned and those enemies of the state not executed toiled away in labour camps until the early 1960s. Building the New Spain dreamed of Franco's regime and the Falange Party, but one of cultural philistinism, in the words of Jeremy Black in *A short history of Spain.*

By 1950, with the economy struggling, Spain was forced to be less isolationist and the United Nations reopened diplomatic relations with Spain. Caught up in a nuclear arms race, anti-communist witch-hunts and McCarthyism, the United States forged closer links with totalitarian Spain. Madrid became a playground for American film stars and the wealthy, while large cities like Madrid, Bilbao and Barcelona attracted thousands to fulfil roles in industry or services.

Although he died in 1975, the memory of Franco is still alive today, although the last commemorative statue of Franco was finally removed from outside Neuvos Ministerios in 2005. However, the commemoration of his death and that of Miguel Primo de Rivera (on the same day 40 years apart) is tolerated by the police each 20th November. Supporters, with straight-armed salutes and singing the anthem of the old Falange party, parade in Plaza Oriente.

Cervantes Monument, Torre de Madrid and Edificio Espana.

View from Edificio Espana (RIU Hotel).

Fundacion Juan March.

Two giant buildings, around the Plaza de Espana, were built to project a progressive image of Franco's regime. In 1953 the tallest building in Spain was the **Edificio Espana**, eclipsed four years later by the tallest skyscraper in Europe, the **Torre de Madrid**, standing at 137 metres. Both were proud symbols of economic recovery after the Civil War. Hotels now, the Espana building has the best 360-degree roof terrace views of Madrid.

Local eats

For a small entrance price (cheaper at off-peak times) you can eat and drink on the roof terrace of the **Edificio Espana (RIU Hotel)** (C. Gran Via).

Local eats

Fundacion Juan March, established by the wealthy banker of the same name in 1955, is an important art foundation with a full and diverse programme of performances, lectures and exhibitions, and an extensive library holding books and resources on Spanish cultural themes. Refreshingly (in a city where many venues are closed on Monday), it's open all week. The downstairs restaurant and coffee shop are very atmospheric and relaxing.

Transition to democracy

In November 1975 upon the death of Franco, and at his behest, Juan Carlos (the grandson of Alfonso XIII) returned from exile in Rome and was proclaimed Juan Carlos I, King of Spain.

In June 1977 elections were held, the first since 1936, with seventy parties contesting 350 seats. A majority was won by a coalition led by the UCD (Unión de Centro Democrático), appointing Pedro Suarez as Prime Minister. Prior to the election, all the main parties agreed to a *Pact of Forgetting* – i.e., not to eradicate the memory or prevent discussion of the Civil War and the Franco period but to agree not to confront or make political capital out of the matters. In the same year, Spain requested membership of the European Economic Community (EEC). And in October 1977, an *Amnesty Law* was passed for all crimes of war and terrorism during and after the Civil War. Some groups like ETA (Basque separatists) regarded the advances as meaningless since they wanted independence. In December 1978, a constitution was drawn up and agreed with all parties (except parties on the extreme left and right), legitimised by public referendum and sanctioned by the king. It embedded democracy and proclaimed, despite being a non-confessional constitution (i.e., where politics and religion do not mix), that Catholicism is the historical religion of the country.

From the 1970s, tourism started to become a significant factor in the economy, and aided by the skill and charm of Seve Ballesteros, Spain became a major worldwide golfing destination. Coupled with a growth in manufacturing and the passing of more progressive laws (such as mandatory education) it was a transformation of fortunes that would later be dubbed the 'Spanish Miracle'.

The shabbiness of the late 1970s gave way to a newly confident and exuberant city, its citizens intent on making up for the decades lost under the dictatorship. The new spirit was embodied in La Movida Madrileña (i.e., The Madrid Scene) – a hedonistic cultural movement spanning the arts, fashion, drugs, alcohol and sexual behaviours. Much of the period is popularised in the films of Pedro Almodovar, many set in Madrid, such as *All About My Mother* and *Talk to Her* – taking on sexual norms and taboos.

Throughout the late 1970s and 1980s, Spain consolidated its position in the international community: accession to NATO in 1979, passing of more progressive laws (e.g., legalising divorce in 1981), membership of the EEC in 1986 (becoming its president in 1989, 1995 and 2002), and adopting the euro in 2002.

Elections in October 1982 saw an absolute majority for the left-wing

PSOE and its leader Felipe González as Prime Minister (PM) – a role also known as President of the Council of Ministers. The PSOE returned to power in June 1986, December 1989 and June 1993, on each occasion under González.

The election of 1996 saw a swing to the right under the Popular Party (PP) and its leader José María Aznar, which consolidated its electoral position in March 2000, then lost to the PSOE (with José Luis Rodríguez Zapatero as PM) in 2004.

In October 2007, the *Historical Memory Law* condemned the repression of the Civil War and gave rights to its victims and descendants – providing in a small way, justice, dignity and moral reparations to the victims of the war. This law was extended in October 2022 with the *Democratic Memory Law*, making it possible for the descendants of those who left Spain during the Civil War to obtain Spanish citizenship.

The 2008 general election was won by the PSOE (with José Luis Rodríguez Zapatero, PM) whilst in 2011, victory swung back to the PP (Mariano Rajoy, PM), and power was retained in 2014 under Rajoy. Also, that year, following allegations of wrong-doing, Juan Carlos abdicated in favour of his son, Felippe VI, who with his wife Queen Letizia and Princesses Leonor and Sofia became Spain's first family.

In October 2017, the leaders of the Catalan Presidency held a public referendum that sought independence for the region. The citizens of Catalan voted in favour, but with a turnout of 43 per cent. A resolution for a Catalan declaration of independence was passed in the Parliament of Catalonia, but with around 30 per cent of MPs abstaining. Ignoring its own legal counsel, the affair was incautious and the declaration received no recognition from the international community. The Madrid Government declared its illegality, and the Catalan leaders went into exile.

In 2018, the PSOE won elections (with Pedro Sanchez, PM) – and retained power in 2024. In a divisive move, the exiled Catalan leaders were offered amnesty in exchange for their votes, thereby securing another term in office for the PSOE Government. Many believed this smacked dangerously of political behaviours that precipitated the Civil War, perpetuating a deep mistrust of political power.

The PSOE is the same party established in 1899 and has had an amazing run of success, holding political power in government longer than any other in modern democratic Spain, withstanding pressures from the centre-right PP and far-right Vox Party. Today, Basque is the most autonomous region, having its own taxes, policing and language taught in school. Catalonia seeks parity.

Today, despite having world-class physical public infrastructure, Spain trails behind in investment in people.

In recent years, temporary contracts are preferred over permanent ones. This produces high unemployment, partly a consequence of seasonal tourism but also the unviable contract severance costs in the private sector. In consequence, the public sector has become bloated, soaking up the unskilled unemployed and tormenting the aspirational young with lengthy civil service entrance examinations (i.e., Oposiciones).

After the 'fat-cow years' between 1996 and 2008, when the bubble of unsustainable construction crashed, many were left in negative equity. And like many countries in Europe, Spain has a looming pension problem.

Today, a lack of visibility about the Civil War and the Franco regime still pervades the national curriculum – silent on the Franco period, resistance to the regime during the Civil War and repression after the war. Many bodies remain unidentified in containers or undiscovered graves. Some elements of the army still praise Franco, and there remains an imbalance of memorials to his regime compared to Republican equivalents. The young, and those on the left, are eager to change this situation. Meanwhile, the conservative Popular Party promotes an image of right-wing Spanish Christian unity and Vox still appeals to the far right, a significant proportion of whom believe the memory of Franco's legacy is judged too harshly.

Difficult constitutional issues remain in the consciousness: for example, the reason Spain is a monarchy (and not a republic) is because Franco willed it. The Spanish national anthem is still denied any lyrics, largely because the various political factions cannot agree on them.

The modern era has brought with it exciting new business opportunities and family attractions. Since its construction in 1996, **Puerta de Europa** (Paseo de la Castellana) has been regarded as one of the classic modern architectural structures in Europe. Appearing to defy gravity, the leaning towers, resembling a modern-day triumphal gate, welcome visitors to Madrid and the **Paseo de la Castellana** – a six-kilometre-long highway of fabled aristocratic homes, corporate headquarters and embassies. The Puerta de Europa has stimulated a host of other tall buildings further north, projecting Madrid into the super-league of modern architecture and construction engineering.

In the west of Madrid, the **Parque de Atracciones** and the **Zoo Aquarium de Madrid** draw large crowds, whilst the nearby **Madrid Rio** provides various free leisure facilities running parallel to the River Manzanares for ten kilometres – a highlight at its centre being the Madrid Rio Beach; a large, serviced picnic area and café with water jets for cooling down in the summer. In the south, **Faunia** exhibits nature and biodiversity

Cuatro Torres, Paseo de la Castellana.

Puerta de Europa.

in eight ecosystem pavilions, from arctic to tropical environments. Further afield, **Parque Warner Madrid** (a theme park) and **Aquopolis** provide land, air and water-based exhilaration for adults and families.

Opened in 2004, the **Museo del Traje** (Museum of Costume) consolidated various smaller garment collections into a coherent national collection, with items dating from the late medieval period to the modern day. Its exhibits include garments from the most important designers of the twentieth century (e.g. Fortuny, Balenciaga and Dior) and encourages a hands-on experience with less valuable garments. The museum is also surrounded by beautiful, landscaped gardens.

Local eats

Museo del Traje has a café and a large restaurant, catering for large groups and popular for Sunday lunch after visiting the collections.

With an operating Royal Court, rich and varied architecture and a proud creative heritage, Madrid is one of few capital cities where history so strongly shapes the culture. Add to this an active political scene, the centre of national government and a tumultuous past, it attracts intellectual and energetic types whether activists, campaigners or trend setters. With copious popular and niche entertainment venues, aided by a two-hour siesta before late-night eating and drinking, Madrid exudes a spirit of non-stop energy, today being driven forward by a young and ambitious generation of Madrileños.

KEY SOURCES AND SELECTED FURTHER READING

Books

Bennett, A. *Explore Madrid – the best routes around the city*. (London: Apa Insight Guides, 2018).

Black, J. *A brief history of Spain*. (London: Robinson, Hachette, 2019).

Day, P. *Franco's Friends – how British intelligence helped bring Franco to power in Spain*. (London: Biteback, 2011).

Holland, J. *Madrid 25 Best*. (Basingstoke: AA Media, 2019).

Jenkins, S. *A short history of Europe – from Pericles to Putin*. (London: Penguin, 2018).

Mendoza, E. *An Englishman in Madrid*. (London: MacLehose, Quercus, 2013, Eng. translation, first pub. 2010).

Nash, E. *Madrid: a cultural and literary companion*. (Oxford: Signal Books, 2001).

Orwell, G. *Homage to Catalonia*. (London: Penguin Random House UK, 2000, first pub. 1938).

Parsons, D. *A cultural history of Madrid: modernism and the urban spectacle*. (Oxford: Berg, 2003).

Preston, P. *The Spanish Civil War – reaction, revolution and revenge*. (London: Collins, 2016, first pub. 2006).

Sansom, C.J. *Winter in Madrid*. (London: Pan, Macmillan, 2016, first pub. 2006).

Stewart, J. *Madrid: a literary guide for travellers*. (London: I. B. Tauris, 2019).

Tremlett, G. *Ghosts of Spain: travels through a country's hidden past* (London: Faber, 2012).

Websites

City of Madrid Tourism, 'Take a look', *esmadrid.com* [online]. Available from: <https://www.esmadrid.com/vistazo-madrid?utm_source=portal&utm_medium=menu_DeunVistazo&utm_campaign=enlace_Menu_DeunVistazo>

La Moncloa, 'History and Culture of Spain', *lamoncloa.gob.es* [online]. Available from: <https://www.lamoncloa.gob.es/lang/en/espana/historyandculture>

INDEX

N

O

P